Staff Library

Effective School Leaders

SCHOOL LEADERSHIP AND MANAGEMENT SERIES

Series Editors: Brent Davies and John West-Burnham

Other titles in the series:

Effective Learning in Schools
by Christopher Bowring-Carr and John West-Burnham

From Bursar to School Business Manager
Fergus O'Sullivan, Angela Thody and Elizabeth Wood

Leadership and Professional Development in Schools
by John West-Burnham and Fergus O'Sullivan

Managing Learning for Achievement
Edited by Christopher Bowring-Carr and John West-Burnam

Managing Quality in Schools (2nd edition)
by John West-Burnham

Middle Management in Schools
by Sonia Blandford

Reengineering and Total Quality in Schools
by Brent Davies and John West-Burnham

Resource Management in Schools
by Sonia Blandford

Strategic Marketing for Schools
by Brent Davies and Linda Ellison

Forthcoming title:

Information and Communication Technology in Schools
by Paul James

Effective School Leaders

How to evaluate and improve your leadership potential

JOHN MACBEATH AND
KATE MYERS

FINANCIAL TIMES
Prentice Hall

An imprint of PEARSON EDUCATION
London · New York · San Francisco · Toronto · Sydney · Tokyo · Singapore ·
Hong Kong · Cape Town · Madrid · Paris · Milan · Munich · Amsterdam ·

PEARSON EDUCATION LIMITED

Head Office:
Edinburgh Gate
Harlow CM20 2JE
Tel: +44 (0)1279 623623
Fax: +44 (0)1279 431059

London Office:
128 Long Acre, London WC2E 9AN
Tel: +44 (0)20 7447 2000
Fax: +44 (0)20 7240 5771
Website: www.business-mind.com

First published in Great Britain 1999

ISBN 0 273 63958 7

British Library Cataloguing in Publication Data
A CIP catalogue record for this book can be obtained from the British Library.

10 9 8 7 6 5 4 3 2

Typeset by Pantek Arts, Maidstone, Kent.
Printed and bound in Great Britain.

The Publishers' policy is to use paper manufactured from sustainable forests.

£16 – 99

Contents

■ ■ ■

Dedicated to
Johnny Thomassen and Dorothy Myers

Acknowledgements

We would like to thank those who contributed to this book. There are many people, too numerous to mention, whose research and writing about leadership have influenced our thinking, and many who provided us with their personal accounts of the triumphs and dilemmas of school leadership. Thanks to Sue Adler and Diana Leonard who read and commented helpfully on Chapter 6, and to Sandra MacBeath, Evelyn Gittoes and Elaine Kirkland who contributed to drafts at various stages of gestation.

1

Competences, Competencies and Context

Leadership. It is vital for teams, for organisations, for countries and even, if we are to believe the popular press, for the world itself. 'The world cries out for firm leadership', said the *Daily Mail* of 31 August 1998, citing the simultaneous crises of Russian and American presidencies. It is at times of crisis – the collapse of the economy, the risk of instability, the threat of war – that people look to leaders to sort things out, to rescue us, to make things right. In a historical study of 35 dictatorships (Hertzler, 1940) it was found that all of them had emerged during times of social distress. Commenting on this need for authority figures, Ronald Heifetz (1994) says that it is when people are 'unhinged from their habits' that they look with the greatest intensity to authority figures for remedies.

Much has been written about 'world leaders', heroic individuals who have shaped the flow of human affairs and left their imprint on the course of history. Their achievements and leadership styles are researched with the purpose of learning lessons which can be applied in other contexts, in personal relationships, in business, in schools. One of the earliest of this genre of researchers was Napoleon Hill, the young journalist commissioned by Carnegie in 1928 to go out and interview 500 notable leaders and to return in 20 years with the completed book. Among the outstanding leaders he wrote about were Woodrow Wilson, Howard Taft, Alexander Graham Bell, Theodore Roosevelt, Thomas Edison and Henry Ford. Many of these were distinguished as much by their idiosyncrasies as by the convergent strands which thread through their differing accounts. But running through all their stories Hill found a core of common characteristics and leading principles.

More recently Howard Gardner (1997) wrote about 'leading minds' of our time and, from biographies as diverse as Mohandas Gandhi, Pope John Paul XXIII, Martin Luther King and Eleanor Roosevelt, sought to draw out the traits which distinguish exemplary leaders. In the language of the management text-book these would be described as 'competen*cies*', that is, qualities that people bring to their task and infuse the job they do with new meaning and direction. These are different and distinct from 'competen*ces*' – the prescriptive repertoire of skills that a job requires.

Competencies and competences

The conceptual difference underlying this technical distinction between 'competences' and 'competencies ' is a fundamental one in the study of leadership. Some people are attracted and others repelled by the terminology. None the less it is crucial to our understanding to separate the analysis that starts with jobs and roles and the analysis that starts with people. Napoleon Hill and Howard Gardner favour this second approach. It looks for people who have distinguished themselves in some significant way as leaders. Having chosen those people and been explicit about criteria for their selection, they then try to identify and understand what took them into positions of leadership, their driving motives, their strengths and frailties.

The competences approach, by contrast, takes as its point of departure the nature of the job to be done, the vacancy to be filled. The competences are, therefore, not free-floating but located in an organisational context with a set of preconditions. Recruitment and selection for headship quite typically exemplifies this. Heads, irrespective of who they are, require subject degree qualifications, teaching certificates, experience of classroom teaching, expertise in managing people, organisational and communications skills and so on. As we move down the competences route these pre-specifications become tighter, more detailed and more objectified.

Much of this is sensible, but we must also recognise that the more pinned down the competences and the more scripted the role, the more we risk precluding the X factor – the surprise, the chemistry, the shift in perspective that may be brought by a candidate who does not fit the arithmetic but may, none the less, bring a magical quality to the leadership task. Despite their failure to meet required competences, they can still bring a freshness of thinking, a personal vision or challenge to the preconceptions of the framemakers.

'Headhunting', another practice imported into education from the business world, may lay emphasis on the competence or the competency model. People may be sought for their special personal qualities or because they appear to meet the competences specification of the job. Most recruitment practice, however, approaches from both directions, attempting to find a closeness of fit between personal competencies, on the one hand, and job competences on the other.

Context

A third dimension, or a third way of looking at leadership in practice, is to move beyond the person and beyond organisational role and status to examine the context in which leadership is exercised. When leadership is viewed in this way, our focus of attention is on the hinterland rather than the foreground. In the process the figure in the foreground may become less distinct, of less immediate interest than the context in which he or she is located. The focus on context has been described in the past as 'situational leadership', based on the view that leaders tend to be creatures and products of their time. So a given set of circumstances coalesces to allow a Gandhi, a Churchill, or a Kennedy to seize the day. On the less dramatic stage of school leadership it is also evident that headteachers, too, are often creatures of time and place.

In order to come to the fullest understanding of school leadership, therefore, we need to examine the range of school and community contexts in which heads are required to lead, and where sometimes they are required to follow. From this perspective we may discover that leadership has many facets and many faces. There is no simple linear relationship between leading and following, between hierarchy and authority, between formal status and personal influence. A Keele University study (Barber and Brighouse, 1992) reported that teachers found the implicit notion of their role as followers inadequate:

> *they are, after all, professionals making decisions in every lesson in ways which they know affect the real business of the school, the learning and development of pupils. Teachers know they make the vital decisions. In a sense they know they are the people who are really leading by example . . . (p. 51)*
>
> *(Brighouse and Woods, 1999)*

The three approaches – competences, competencies and context – may be characterised as the who, what and where – 'Who make good leaders?' 'What kind of leaders do we want?' and 'Where can leadership be found?' We examine each of these in turn.

Who make good leaders?

Among the qualities found in exemplary leaders (seven men, three women) identified by Howard Gardner were:

- a readiness to confront authority
- risk-taking
- resilience in the face of failure

- confidence in one's own instinct and intuition
- the ability to see and keep in mind the big picture
- being driven by a moral commitment
- a sense of timing, allowing one to stand back, reflect and learn from experience.

Gardner (1997) writes:

> *The capacity to take risks speaks to a confidence that one will at least sometimes attain success; implacability in the face of opposition likewise reflects a willingness to rely on oneself and not to succumb to others' strictures and reservations. (p. 33)*

These larger-than-life leaders were marked out by their ability to strike out in new directions, with enough self-confidence to ignore the forces of inertia and conservatism pushing them back to shallower waters. They also had the inner resilience to confront the possibility of failure and recrimination. These are not the kind of competences that are easy to define or prescribe. They are qualities that reside deeply within individual experience and express themselves most cogently at times of critical decision-making. The competencies approach owes much to the American group known as McBer. They studied leaders in a range of different occupational contexts (Spencer and Spencer, 1993) including medicine, the military, social services and education. The 360 distinctive items of personal behaviour which they identified were conflated to produce 20 competencies (Figure 1.1). These were described by McBer as 'generic compe-

Achievement and action • achievement orientation • concern for order • information seeking • initiative	Helping and human service • interpersonal understanding • customer service orientation
Managerial • developing others • directiveness • teamwork and co-operation	Cognitive • analytical thinking • team leadership • conceptual thinking • technical/professional expertise
Impact and influence • influence • organisational awareness • relationship building	Personal effectiveness • self-control • self-confidence • flexibility • organisational commitment

Figure 1.1: McBer's generic competencies
(*Source*: Spencer and Spencer, 1993)

tencies' because, it was claimed, they apply across the whole range of contexts in which leadership is exercised.

One of the distinguishing qualities of leaders which emerged from one of the early McBer studies (Spencer, 1978) was 'rule-breaking'. Even within the rigid structures of the military, rule-breaking appeared to be the key to success. It might even be argued that the more authoritarian or the more bureaucratic the structure, the greater the premium on rule-breaking. There is an echo of this in Gardner's research and an interesting parallel in Boylett and Finlay's (1996) survey of 1000 headteachers. They identified one of the most important characteristics of the successful headteacher to be 'a healthy disrespect of authority'. To describe disrespect for authority as 'healthy' is provocative but a reminder of the unhealthy respect which has historically led people down a perilous path.

The deviousness needed to circumvent authority and constraining formal systems of control brings into sharp focus the difference between competencies and competences. No set of job descriptors would be likely to identify disrespect for authority, rule-breaking and deviousness as desirable competences, since they are by definition antithetical to the requirements of any rule-bound organisation. At least on the surface. Yet when we turn to the educational leaders who left a mark on history it is often by virtue of those very subversive qualities.

The upsetting of conventional wisdom was the hallmark of educational heretics such as Sanderson of Oundle, Arnold of Rugby and Neill of Summerhill, all of whom shook the conventions and foundations of schooling in their respective eras. There are many accounts of larger-than-life headteachers and smaller-than-life schools which failed to accommodate to one another. A famous Scottish dominie and contemporary of Neill, R.F. Mackenzie, published prolifically in the 1960s under such titles as *Escape from the Classroom* and *The Unbowed Head*, yet like others before and after him, he came famously unstuck within the state sector. Without the freedom of reign enjoyed by Arnold, Neill and Sanderson in the independent sector, Mackenzie found it impossible to follow his principles through at Aberdeen's (ironically named) Summerhill Academy. His attempts to abolish corporal punishment were a rule-break too far, given the deeply institutionalised approach to chastisement in the Scottish culture at that time.

A close parallel in yet another 'hill site' – Risinghill in Islington – was the high-profile demise of Michael Duane who, like Mackenzie, put principles before pragmatics. In retrospect we might describe Mackenzie and Duane as having the competencies of potentially great leaders, but out of their time – visionaries without the competences of compromise.

David Winkley (1989) says in relation to Michael Duane:

> *It is not good enough for the leader merely to fashion enlightened ideas. There were forty-nine teachers pro-Duane, and twenty-nine against; the opposition was too great for progress by imposition. What Duane needed was not ideas, but strategies. (p. 23)*

Without strategy, vision has no momentum. Without vision, strategy leads to a mundane place. David Winkley goes on to say about democratic leadership:

> *The argument here is that democracy, with the careful understanding of its meaning in the context of the school, is something a leader needs to work towards if he wishes the school and the staff to grow and develop their full potential. There must, however, be two essential qualifications. First that the head can never absolve himself at any stage in his leadership from the responsibility of leadership. Secondly, that democracy has to be understood in relation to accountability; that is to say, the 'democracy' of the staff decision making process needs to be seen in relation to wider questions of democracy for parents, children, and the community at large. (p. 23)*

In Chapter 3 we look in more detail at a group of 27 headteachers and attempt to plot some of the common attributes they brought to their jobs. The differences among them are in some respects as strong as the similarities which unite them. They have in common a desire to be democratic and collaborative, but recognise that this is relative to the expectations which others hold, the stage of growth of the school as an organisation and the stage in their own personal and professional development. They are aware of the fluidity of competencies and their juxtaposition, often in delicate balance. As one of these secondary heads says:

> *Knowing when to push and when to back off, when to give strong lead and when to support. Different situations and different times need different approaches.*

Another head describes personal qualities which might be hard to encapsulate in competences language – 'a sensitive heart but the skin of a rhinoceros'.

Schools that have involved children in the interviewing of candidates for headship have found that pupils' spontaneous untutored questions go naturally beyond the obvious job competences and beyond the formal role to the personal and human issues. Children ask candidates about themselves and about their lives outside school. What, for example, did they like doing when they were not being a teacher? What were their hobbies? Did they have pets or pet hates? While none of these qualify easily as competences, they are, from a child's eye view, revealing. What these children were looking for was, as one pupil put it, 'the inside person'. A Scottish primary school which involved children in the selection of teachers reported that the pupils' selection was made primarily on the basis of the candidate who took the greatest interest in them and their work and used their first names when talking to them.

What kind of leaders do we want?

In common practice the kind of leaders we look for tend to be viewed from the perspective of the job they are required to do, and our expectations of them are shaped by our past experience of those who previously occupied the role. When we elect prime ministers and presidents we fit them into the mould of successful prior incumbents. American presidents, for example, have, with only one or two exceptions, been white Protestant men over six feet tall. There is an in-built phenotype, a conservative inertia which defines the parameters of the role, provides the frame for what we see and furnishes the terminology of our thinking.

This conservatism operates powerfully in relation to school leadership. We look for certain job qualities that have proved themselves in the past. These tend to be similar, whatever perspective they are viewed from – national policy-makers, local authorities, governors, parents, teachers or students. Perhaps, as Gerald Grace (1995) argued, this is because a deeply ingrained public school imagery of headship has shaped our conceptions of the role:

> *although formed in the exclusive context of upper-class education in England, it can be seen to have had significant cultural and pedagogic mediations in other sectors of English schooling. Its construct of school leadership and its culture of headship as personal, powerful, controlling, moralising and patriarchal has become an important constituent in the subsequent discourse and practice of school headship. (p. 11)*

Competences from a pupil perspective

However much they look for the 'inside person' in their selection of a new head, children are also inherently conservative in their descriptions of competences. Their view of headship is determined almost exclusively by what they see and know from direct first-hand experience. This can be illustrated from the Effective Leadership study (MacBeath, 1998) in which we asked six- and seven-year-olds to draw and write about their headteachers. Many portrayed their heads as sitting in their office, thinking, reading or on the telephone. An equally large number portrayed their headteachers leading the singing or playing the piano. These were illuminating sources of evidence, illustrating the contexts in which children met and 'framed' their heads, in assemblies or behind the office door marked 'headteacher'.

Some of the children depicted heads visiting classes, often to say 'well done' or to hand out sweets. Young children accepted these roles at face value while their teachers read into these a deeper, and sometimes more sinister, intent.

Danish teachers were the most antagonistic to surprise visits, seeing them as 'spying on colleagues'. Yet pupils in those same Danish schools placed a positive value on this and wrote statements such as 'The job of good heads is to ensure that teachers are teaching well.' This illustrates the usefulness of alternative viewpoints on the headteacher role and the value of the 'worms-eye view' in challenging more conservative and egocentric perspectives.

Despite their inherent conservatism as 'insiders' of the system, children and young people provide another lens from which to view leadership. If children were more likely than their teachers to emphasise the overseeing role of the head, this could be explained by their more varied and multi-faceted experience of school. In secondaries in particular they had a broader intuitive understanding of the variabilities and vagaries of the many teachers they met on a day-to-day basis. Students, as we have found in many studies, are much more keenly attuned to issues of fairness and equality than their teachers, and for them this arbitration in the life of the school community by a headteacher was most highly valued. A Scottish nine-year-old wrote:

> *She should treat all pupils fairly and make sure that teachers act fairly as well. It is her job to make sure teachers act correctly because they are not all fair.*

Among the list of qualities, or 'competences', for heads mentioned by primary pupils were:

- accepts complaints
- pays attention to unhappy kids
- doesn't use the rod
- talks about the good news
- cheers you up
- protects education
- keeps the playground tidy
- has music/sporting skills
- is good with bad children, for example, keeping them in at playtime
- posting letters to parents of very bad children.

Older primary children, with a greater breadth of experience and often keen perceptiveness, wrote about their heads in these terms:

> *A headteacher has to make learning as fun as possible so children will want to learn. She has to make sure we have all the resources we need to do our work.*

> *A headteacher is the foundation of the school. Without a headteacher there would be caous.*

He/she will make sure the school is a nice place for the children and the people who work there. They help the school have a good reputation.

Secondary students tended to lay greater emphasis on the human side of leadership. The largest cluster of 'competences' identified by secondary age students were:

- listens
- talks with pupils
- is nice/kind to pupils
- takes care of pupils
- understands pupils
- someone you can trust
- establishes good relationships
- has a sense of humour
- is accessible/approachable
- doesn't shout at you
- is loyal to pupils/staff.

Taken together, these may be categorised as 'establishing positive relationships,' which for older students is manifestly the most important criterion of good headship. There is an interesting juxtaposition of this with 'strictness', a quality frequently mentioned by English and Scottish students but not once among the 146 statements made by the Danes. For the UK students there were no apparent contradictions in this but there is a caveat, expressed in these terms by a Scottish student: 'A good head is someone who is strict when he needs to be but righteous in his judicial decisions.' Indeed, as with the primary pupils, the second largest cluster of qualities of good heads had to do with fairness, justice and equality.

Other aspects of the role, such as being 'financially knowledgeable' or 'good with money', only figure occasionally in students' lists of competences. Given that there is a greater degree of financial local management of schools in England, it is perhaps surprising that secondary students in English schools failed to mention this aspect of the head's role at all. For them the emphasis was almost entirely on the nature of relationships and personal qualities that a good head should exemplify. Analysis of pupils' writing and incidence of key phrases was recorded and ranked by the research team. From a total of over 50 phrases from each country, a top ten was compiled. These are shown in Figures 1.2 and 1.3.

	Denmark	*No. of phrases*	**England**	*No. of phrases*	**Scotland**	*No. of phrases*
1	Kind	29	Tells children off if they're naughty	45	Is nice/kind	59
2	Sympathetic	7	Good organiser	42	Ensures there is no bullying	43
3	Keeps school orderly	7	Helps teacher/ children	25	Sense of humour/good fun	37
4	Tells children off if they're naughty	7	Buys things for the school	25	Strict/good discipline	36
5	Solves problems	6	Runs the school properly	22	Understanding	32
6	Arranges good outings	6	Sorts out arguments/ problems	21	Helpful	29
7	Happy	6	Friendly to parents	15	Happy/cheerful	24
8	Good to kids	4	Teaches classes	15	Treats children fairly	23
9	Walks the school	4	Praises children	11	Likes children	22
10	Keeps the school clean	2	Makes sure children are OK/safe	11	Listens to what we have to say	21

Figure 1.2: Primary pupils' responses to questions regarding what a head does and what a good head is like

	Denmark	*No. of phrases*	***England***	*No. of phrases*	***Scotland***	*No. of phrases*
1	Listens	37	Fair	16	Listens	67
2	Talks with pupils	36	Good relationships with pupils/ teachers	9	Is understanding	55
3	Kind	30	Accessible/ approachable	7	Treats children fairly	46
4	Nice to pupils	29	Caring	7	Strict/good discipline	45
5	Treats pupils equally	24	Understands pupils	7	Someone to talk to/talks to us	45
6	Keeps school nice, clean/ orderly	23	Takes account of pupils' opinions	6	Good relationships with pupils	44
7	Takes care of pupils	19	Good listener	6	Sense of humour/good fun	35
8	Manages the school	16	Responsible	5	Looks after/ capable of running school	27
9	Respectable	15	Treats people equally	5	Is nice/kind	24
10	Understands pupils	14	Maintains discipline	4	Not too strict	21

Figure 1.3: Older students' responses to the question 'What is a good headteacher?'

A parental view of competences

As with pupils, parents' views might be expected to reflect what they were familiar with from their own experience. But, like students, they emphasise above all else the human qualities, the interpersonal skills such as communication, empathy, accessibility, and the ability to motivate and inspire young people. In common with their children, they wanted headteachers to be accessible, approachable and open. They wanted discipline too and, while less liable to mention fairness and equality, they did make the link between discipline and morality, stressing the moral authority of the headteacher and her adjudicator role. The head was often seen by parents as the final arbiter among different stakeholders, understanding and even-handed, representing and responding fairly to differing interests. The emphasis on consistency and fairness was perhaps an indication of the importance attached to the adjudicator role.

The supervision and professional development of staff was a related issue and also came high on the list of parental priorities:

> *The head has to know what's going on and I would want him to make sure he passes that on. Like professional development – it's to the advantage of the pupils that the teachers know about new methods and the head needs to ensure they're up-to-date. He needs to ensure information is coming in from the outside and the place isn't stagnating.*

Of all groups it was the Danish parents who were most likely to mention the role of the headteacher as professional developer. They did not want their heads to be in the front line, teaching classes; but behind the teachers, motivating and encouraging them to keep their knowledge and expertise up to date. As with students, money and resource management took a back seat. Although parents were more likely to mention it and see its importance, they also saw it as much less significant than personal relationships and people management:

> *For a headteacher this [managing the budget] should come quite low down; children and people should come before money. I'd rather a school had poor resources but a good atmosphere than good resources and a poor atmosphere.*

Competences from the teacher's perspective

Being a good communicator was the quality identified as most important from the teacher's point of view. This did not, however, refer to the competences of the headteacher as a persuasive speaker, an effective memo writer or manager of communication systems. What teachers placed most value on was the ability of the head to listen to others:

The previous head knew what he wanted and made a bee line straight for it. He was not deterred by what we thought or anyone thought, for that matter. He was the world's worst listener. When we were looking for a new head I said to our teacher rep on the School Board, 'I don't care whether he or she wears purple tights and has three heads . . . all I want is a good listener'.

The importance of accurate, or empathic, listening is not easy to dissect in terms of specific competences. The constituent parts do not come together to make a whole, yet there is evidence to suggest that effective listeners do a number of identifiable things. They are able to achieve an accurate grasp of the content, the meaning and the feeling. In behavioural terms they:

- can repeat accurately what was said;
- identify correctly the feelings lying behind the words;
- identify correctly the meaning that the word and feelings have for the person concerned.

There is an interesting gender dimension to this set of skills which we deal with in more depth in Chapter 6, but attempts to pin down some of these competences simply underline the significance of their less tangible and elusive qualities. This theme is taken up by the researchers Cave and Wilkinson (1997) who tried to find a way of describing some of the more subjective competences of leadership. They identified four 'higher order' skills which they described as 'reading the situation', 'intuition', 'balanced judgement' and 'political acumen'. 'Reading the situation' they described as 'keeping antennae out' and 'picking up vibes', not very precise in terms of behavioural competences and clearly difficult to train for, but cerebral activities that neurology is helping us to identify with greater precision. Thanks to thermal imaging technology, these once elusive skills can be revealed as having an identifiable locus in the emotional centres of the brain.

David Hargreaves (1997), writing about 'social intelligence', says:

social intelligence, the ability and sensitivity to understand and predict other people's mind and intentions, and behave skillfully in social relationships – has always been highly esteemed by employers. It is now seen by some evolutionary biologists and social scientists as the root of all *intellectual development. (p. 3)*

In his book *What's Worth Fighting for in the Principalship?* Michael Fullan (1997a) offers four apparently simple precepts – maintaining focus, making your position clear to those above you, managing time accordingly, and saying no. None of these is possible to prescribe in any set of competences because they rely so heavily on social intelligence. They rely not only on reading the situation correctly, but then acting on that reading in a way sensitive enough to convey authority while supporting the authority of the other(s) in the relationship.

One of the headteachers in the Effective Leadership study (MacBeath, 1998) described a simple precept given to him by a predecessor – 'Don't ask about the parrot'. As illustrated in Figure 1.4, however conspicuous the parrot, only by ignoring it will you prevent it from being transferred to your own shoulder. While admitting the wisdom of the counsel, this headteacher had found that it was not after all a simple precept, but one that called not for a blind eye, but a very far-seeing one.

These 'soft skill competencies', as McBer describes them, contrast sharply with some of the hard-edged competences of the management literature and with some of the tenets and assumptions of 'new public management'. They do not sit comfortably with the emphasis on 'strong' leadership, in which strength appears to be equated with single-mindedness, intransigence and 'managing' people so as to align them with the mission or vision of the organisation. Some of the headteachers whose accounts are given in Chapter 3 spoke of the necessity for strong leadership yet, while valuing listening as an important leadership skill, seemed compelled to add a disclaimer to the effect that this should not be seen as 'soft' or 'wimpish'.

Figure 1.4: The parrot

In the United Kingdom people are increasingly being appointed to headteacher roles by virtue of their perceived capacities for 'turning the school round'. This evokes an image of a ship steaming off in the wrong direction and requiring to be set on a totally new course, presupposing someone with the requisite strength, authority and singleness of purpose to achieve this. For the Danes in the Effective Leadership study this was a disquieting image. The continual reference to 'strong' leadership struck an alien and disturbing note with them. It was particularly disliked when used to refer to a conferred position within the school hierarchy. Titles such as 'Head of', 'Senior' and 'Manager' were notably missing from the Danish vocabulary, with preference for terms such as 'Chair' or 'Co-ordinator', terms indicative of a more collaborative form of organisation. They laid much greater emphasis on school leaders maintaining and preserving the school culture through collaborative effort within the traditionally Danish, flat structure and through a culture of collegiality which has deep historic and cultural roots. For the researchers it was much harder to see any personification of leadership among the headteachers of the Danish Folkskole, but by virtue of this there were greater opportunities for what we might call 'contextual leadership'.

Contextual leadership

The focus in the literature, in research and in policy-making on the person of the head reveals a lot about how we frame our view of leadership. Much of management training takes as its central focal point the person, the role and their interrelationship. While both competence and competency approaches have validity and utility, there is always the danger of missing the woods for the trees. Studying the ecology of the woodland will often tell a far more compelling story.

One way of looking at leadership is through real situations which call for someone to take a lead, to show initiative, to mobilise others. Some examples are:

- A group of people stand on the bank of the river watching someone drowning.
- A fire has broken out and people are rushing around helpless and confused.
- A group of young people sit around aimlessly, arguing about what to do, where to go.
- Someone has been knocked down in the street. Everyone is trying to help but has anyone called an ambulance? Does anyone know first aid?
- A hill-walking party is hopelessly lost and none more so than the guide.
- On a school trip some of the boys are using racist language. The teacher in charge appears oblivious.

Assuming leadership in these situations will mean taking the initiative, organising other people, bringing order out of chaos, finding a structure amidst the confusion. It may, in some of the instances suggested above, mean usurping the authority or control of people with more formal leadership status. The imperative of action is the impetus to leadership.

In these situations leadership is spontaneous. Permission is not sought but is implicitly granted by those who failed to exercise it. The status of leader is self-conferred among a group of equals – *primus inter pares*. Or, as in some of the examples above, formal authority is ignored and informal leadership is taken, perhaps implicitly granted by others or explicitly resisted by them. Where people follow, it is often gratefully, because they have been relieved of the responsibility of deciding for themselves, because they themselves lacked the knowledge or skill, or perhaps because they didn't have a clear vision of the likely outcome.

This informal character of leadership is important to keep in mind when it comes to examining an organisation such as the school. Schools are not simply planned and ordered places in which the pyramidal hierarchy of power has a one-to-one relationship with the exercise of leadership on a day-to-day basis. In schools accidents happen, fires break out, people go on field trips and get lost and they sometimes drown. Newspapers carry stories of heroic leadership from unexpected quarters or dereliction of leadership by 'people who should have known better'. And on a much more mundane level, acquiescence to, or struggles for, leadership are played out in classrooms, playgrounds, lunch halls, toilets and staff rooms.

It is deceptively easy to start and to end the discussion of leadership by reference solely to this formal organisational context. Much of what we read about school leadership does, in fact, refer to the functioning at a given locus within the organisation, whether in a school or business enterprise. The hierarchy of position and status tends to be taken as a given, and the point of entry for the study of leadership is with the person or persons occupying the highest formal position. Leadership is seen as located at the top and passed down through each successive layer, while those at the bottom of the hierarchy have assumed the role of followers.

This is a form of conditioning which undermines people's own personal authority and capacity for leadership. Ronald Heifetz (1994) suggests that:

> *Many of us have been so conditioned to defer to authority that we do not realise the extent to which we are the source of the authority's power. We forget that we are the principals. (p. 58)*

He adds:

> *Habitually seeking solutions from people in authority is maladaptive. Indeed it is perhaps the essence of maladaptive behaviour. The flight to authority is particularly dangerous . . . because it disables some of our most important personal and collective resources for accomplishing adaptive work. (p. 73)*

Conceptions of leadership which refer to hierarchical authority need to be constantly challenged. Thanks to an evolving literature and the practice of exemplary schools, we are offered new lenses through which to test our own preconceptions. This is what is meant by the term 'reframing', a new perspective brought about by virtue of how the borders and setting of the picture allow us to see its contents quite differently.

Bolman and Deal (1991) in their book *Reframing Organisations,* suggest that we have tended to concentrate too much on the actors and not enough on the stage where the action takes place. They propose that instead of thinking in terms of 'leaders make things happen' we should consider the corollary – 'things make leaders happen'. When we take this perspective we come to realise that leaders are not necessarily prime movers. The story doesn't always start with them. Rather, they enter the stage at some point in the action and are as much shaped by the unfolding drama as shaping it.

Brighouse and Woods (1999) describe teachers as 'the real leaders in the everyday business of schooling'. These exemplary leaders are not *created* by their headteachers, but discovered. Brighouse and Woods quote a study in which they asked pupils to nominate teachers who exercised classroom leadership and received 450 nominations for one teacher. The primary quality of this teacher was 'as developers of other people's skills, actions and beliefs' (p. 49). As in a sequence of Chinese boxes, headteachers and senior management nurture the conditions in which teachers can be leaders while teachers in turn exercise stewardship so that their students can take up the running.

In the Effective Leadership study, Australian secondary students wrote about leadership in quite different terms from their European counterparts. For them the sharing of school leadership was a dominant theme. Neil Dempster and Lloyd Logan (1998), who conducted the Australian part of the study, commented:

> *Students perceived a lack of leadership opportunities for members of the school community other than the principal. Students thought that the responsibility of leadership should be extended to include staff, parents and, more often, students. Indeed, most student responses advocated participation of students in school leadership irrespective of age. Their tone ranges from rational suggestion to direct demand. Three examples illustrate the point.*
>
> *Quite often the leadership of schools is determined by teachers, with minimum input from students. This needs to be changed so that the students have a lot more say.*
>
> *I think that a strong leadership team consists of student leaders, teachers, Deputy Principal and parents.*
>
> *Generally I think that leadership in schools is concentrated too highly in the people high in the hierarchy of schools. I think that leadership opportunities should exist in the staff and with all students in all year levels. (p. 84)*

There is an apocryphal anecdote about the inspector who, in his final report, comments that 'in this school the teachers are doing all the work while their pupils do none'. It is probably a quite common observation because it is so endemic to the structure of schools as we know them. Brighouse and Woods, (1999) conclude, with reference to teacher and student involvement:

> *The work, like the responsibility, has to be shared. Unless the responsibility is shared, however, the bank account of credit in work will soon run dry. They haven't got a stake in where the school is going. (p. 50)*

The bank account metaphor is an apt one. Steven Covey (1989) writes about the 'emotional bank account' that is the investment we have in relationships and teamwork. This is where the motivation, generosity and goodwill lie. This is where the investment in shared leadership pays off. Within hierarchical structures there is a tension between the leadership conferred by the organisation and that which is exercised in spite of the hierarchy. Fluid contextual leadership means being alive to, and embracing, opportunities for people at every level to take the initiative and for headteachers to lead as and when and where appropriate.

This daring, risk-taking notion of shared leadership has too often been sacrificed at the altar of systems management. While there are those who see the distinction between management and leadership as a spurious one, the current of events and their impact has served to sharpen our awareness of the distinctions and their vital importance. Management and leadership may indeed, as critics argue, be integrally and inseparably related but there exist not only two separate words in our vocabulary but two underpinning conceptual worlds and two distinctively real worlds in practice.

The literature is replete with tables distinguishing management from leadership. They sometimes risk presenting cliched and facile dichotomies but it is, none the less, worth looking at these distinctions with a critical eye to see whether or not they stand up to scrutiny. John Kotter (1996, p. 11) proposes the distinction shown in Figure 1.5.

This is not a definitive list but one way of conceptualising the differences, and may be used as a starting-point for a school to evaluate its own approach to management and leadership. (See Figure 1.6.)

Management	*Leadership*
• planning and budgeting • controlling and problem-solving • organising and staffing	• establishing direction • aligning people • motivating and inspiring

Figure 1.5: The management/leadership distinction

Leadership	*Management*
•	•
•	•
•	•
•	•
•	•

Figure 1.6: What are the key differences in your school?

Steven Covey (Covey and Merrill, 1994, p. 36) depicts leadership and management, in a sense, as left and right hands – 'leadership decides what "first things" are, it is management that puts them first – day by day: moment by moment'. In this model leadership is the sifting through and prioritisation among values and competing priorities, thereafter passing the job over to the order-loving systematic manager-within-the-leader. In our experience the relationship is rarely that neat. In the Effective Leadership study there were inspirational leaders who were relatively bad managers and effective managers who relied on others for leadership. There were also successful teams who shared the responsibility of management and leadership, complementing one another.

It is vital to recognise that management is, by definition, expected to produce a degree of predictability and order, to meet the short-term expectations of stakeholder groups, to plan and to work to a more or less rational model. Leadership is more at home in the world of the unpredictable, the spontaneous and creative. The popularity of management and the predominant focus on managerialism in the literature is, Kotter (1996) argues, because management is easier to teach than leadership. Information systems, time management, finance and planning can be taught. Heightened efficiency can be measured and shown to work. People can save time and energy through efficient management. It is therefore not too surprising that management training has developed into such a major industry. Leadership, on the other hand, which is more about people, relationships, intuition, values and moral judgement, is hard to teach because these things are in themselves not easy to identify and difficult to dissect. The attendant danger is that the energy invested in efficient management may be purchased at the expense of leadership

The now dated managerial literature holds that effective organisations demand systematic supervision and monitoring. Indeed, this was the underpinning philosophy of inspectorial systems from time immemorial and is seen in its most contemporary guise in OFSTED. The term 'supervision', says Sergiovanni (1998, p. 42) 'has a negative tinge that conjures up factory images of "snoopervising" foremen checking up on workers'. It is not surprising, therefore, if teachers, who regard themselves as professionals, resent what they see as an intrusive and controlling practice. However, Sergiovanni does go on to discuss the original meaning of 'supervision', which has more of a flavour of stewardship. Exercised well, it means creating opportunities for pupils, teachers and parents to face their problems and take the initiative in solving them. Sergiovanni uses the term 'empowerment' to describe this form of stewardship. Yet it is a word that has become overused and devalued, as well as misused. Two American authors, Binney and Williams (1997) argue that you cannot 'empower' people but you can disempower them very easily by the normal everyday workings of the organisation. They go on:

> *You will really begin to change, take initiative, take risks, provide real feedback, when people have opportunities to learn from mistakes and accept responsibility for what they are doing, when they feel sufficiently confident to do so and are provided with a clear framework . . . Achieving this type of relationship is not easy. It requires much effort, openness and willingness to learn – and some humility. It feels uncomfortable, particularly for leaders in organisations where this style is not the norm. It requires a high degree of self-belief and a willingness to try. (p. 69)*

Lao Tzu, the Chinese sage, put it most eloquently. Perhaps he was thinking of schools when he wrote those often-quoted words:

> *Go to the people*
> *Live among them*
> *Start with what they know*
> *And when the deed is done*
> *The mission accomplished*
> *Of the best leaders*
> *The people will say*
> *We did it*
> *Ourselves.*

Appendix 1.1
Common points of agreement on the good headteacher

In the Effective Leadership study (MacBeath, 1998) there was, across all stakeholder groups and across all four countries consensus that:

- The headteachers' first and foremost commitment should be to their school. That meant being in and around the school, monitoring its everyday life. Their role in the community or on the larger national stage was given low priority.
- School leaders should have a vision for their school. What 'vision' meant was, however, not exactly the same for different countries. While English and Scottish parents wanted a strong hands-on leader who would lead from the front, the Danes and Australians wanted their leaders to be more collaborative. Danish teachers understood 'vision' to mean an ongoing dialogue between the headteacher and staff, as well as other involved groups, about the future direction of the school, building a vision in concert with teachers. This was consistent with descriptions of the head's desirable characteristics – 'loyal', 'humane', 'engaged' and 'co-operative'. The image of leader as manager was generally unpopular, but most unpopular of all with the Danes.
- School leaders should be approachable and have good communication skills. Communications skills were, however, much less frequently mentioned by the Danes, perhaps because leadership operates within flatter structures in which the head's communication skills are less evident and less important.
- While less of a priority with students, teachers, governors and parents were agreed that the head should encourage and motivate staff to keep up to date professionally.
- In all countries students gave high priority to headteachers treating them fairly and equally and ensuring a climate of equal treatment. Instilling a sense of order and discipline was given much greater emphasis by the English and Scots than by the Australians and Danes.

Appendix 1.2
Headteacher competencies – a view from the Industrial Society

The Industrial Society produced its own list of headteacher competencies. They tend to fall into clusters. Five are specifically concerned with 'the human side', recognising the importance of support and encouragement and minimising anxiety:

- supporting other people
- recognising individual effort
- promoting other people's self-esteem
- developing other people
- minimising anxiety.

Three, closely linked to the above, have to do with the leader as reflective and empathic listener:

- seeking to understand before making judgements
- listening to individual ideas and problems
- actively encouraging feedback.

One, which might be seen as a consequence or overarching principle for all of the foregoing, is about empowerment:

- giving those doing the work the power to make decisions.

Three of the 20 refer to personal modelling of behaviour:

- demonstrating personal integrity
- practising what they preach
- showing enthusiasm.

Four fall more into the directive category, in which the leader takes a pro-active role in decision-making and target-setting:

- providing direction
- taking decisions
- agreeing targets
- promoting understanding of the key issues.

Three are about managing change:

- looking at possible future challenges
- encouraging new ways of doing things
- treating mistakes as learning opportunities.

One is explicitly about teamworking:

- encouraging teamwork.

2

Putting Organisations to Work

> *It was the best of times, it was the worst of times. It was the age of wisdom, it was the age of foolishness. It was the epoch of belief, it was the epoch of incredulity. It was the season of light, it was the season of darkness. It was the spring of hope, it was the winter of despair. We had all before us, we had nothing before us.*
>
> *(Dickens,* A Tale of Two Cities*)*

It is as true of the new millennium years as it was of Charles Dickens's mid-eighteenth century. We are living in an age of two paradigms. One is pushing us back towards a mythical past; the other towards a wholly unforeseeable future. It is 'back' to basics, as if in some distant golden age we were all taught to be numerate and literate. Whole-class teaching, setting and selection are promoted as if they had somehow proved themselves in the past. Toughening up and tightening up, more supervision and control are advocated alongside exhortations to produce self-driven lifelong learners, professional teachers, self-improving, 'full-service', 'fresh start' and 'new community' schools. We read about change management, about future-oriented, flexible and creative leadership, but the political context for these seems to leave less and less room for flexibility, spontaneity and originality.

If Dickens had been more fluent in the language of modern management he might have described these opposing currents as a 'force field'. Plagiarised by management theorists from physics, the force field can be illustrated with a simple graphic. To one side of the school are forces helping to push it forward towards its goals, on the other side are the counteracting and constraining forces pushing it back (see Figure 2.1).

Figure 2.1: The force field acting on the school

This device is used in management training to help people to clarify what they see as the brakes and accelerators acting on their organisation. Figure 2.2 is an example of how one headteacher depicted his situation.

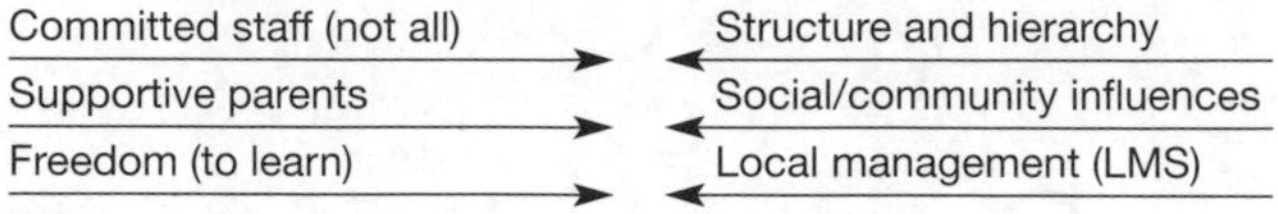

Figure 2.2: One headteacher's brakes and accelerators

The three 'brakes' identified by this headteacher may be seen as operating at three levels: (1) at the level of the structures and hierarchies of the schools as we know them; (2) the community level with its socio-economic capital as a given; (3) the school itself, with its financial parameters and performance targets. On the positive side, the three sets of accelerators refer primarily to people – staff , students and parents – who represent the major resource for change and improvement – the intellectual, emotional and energy capital of the school.

Examining each of these brakes and accelerators in turn may help us to see how an organisation can be put to work more effectively.

The brake of structure and hierarchy

Schools have for decades successfully resisted attempts to change their structure. There is a voluminous critique of the compartmentalised 'egg crate' school and there have been many bold attempts to break up the egg crates and to create more democratic learner-friendly organisations. When this movement of ideas crossed one bridge too far, into deschooling society (Illich, 1971), there was a rapid return of the pendulum, swinging back to the tried, trusted and instantly recognisable models of school. The 'progressive', 'child-centred' schools of the sixties and seventies were deemed to have been a failure, and the open-plan integrated-day primary schools of Oxfordshire and Berkshire ceased to attract the American teachers who had visited them in droves in the early seventies. In Leicestershire the radical innovations of community colleges retreated to a safer, more familiar, set of structures. Reschooling, as it was known, was a systematic concerted retreat to the safer ground of 'real schools'.

The defining landmark in the move backwards to the safety of structure and hierarchy was the Rutter Report, *Fifteen Thousand Hours* (1979). It defined, as two decades of effectiveness studies were to do thereafter, the essential structural features of effective schools – orderly climate, high expectations, achievement-oriented policy, co-operative atmosphere, time on task, and reinforcement and streaming. With the benefit of two decades of hindsight these features appear bland, vague and contestable by turn. Yet their impact has been incredibly far-reaching. Michael Rutter and his team could not have foreseen where this seminal study was to lead, and some members of that team have since been publicly highly critical of the cherry-picking, selective use made of it by politicians and policy-makers. None the less, Rutter's and other school effectiveness studies offered to policy-makers irresistibly neat blueprints for the monitoring and evaluation of schools. These included indicators and performance criteria by which schools could be held to account. The studies appeared to satisfy the need for some clear and simple answers, and showed that research does not always have to be tentative, equivocal, ambiguous and impenetrable. Following on from Rutter, school effectiveness studies consistently singled out 'strong leadership' as a key constituent and reaffirmed the place of the headteacher in the structural hierarchy.

The hierarchical nature of school, as in many other types of organisation, not only frames our view of leadership but, by its very nature, contributes to what Peter Senge (1992) has called 'organisational learning disabilities'. These are a consequence of a mind-set and the accompanying processes which, Senge argues, conspire to defraud the business enterprise, the public agency or the school, of its own innate potential and latent capacity for shared leadership.

How organisations become disabled

Learning disabilities are often a function of hierarchies, even in organisations which appear to require such structure. The most unadulterated form of this can be seen in the military hierarchy, as portrayed by Hollywood in films such as *Full Metal Jacket*, *The Hill*, *An Officer and a Gentleman*. These films depict new recruits being systematically stripped of initiative, individuality and independence of thought and action. This takes place first and foremost through training to conform and obey, but it is also seen as the first step in preparation for leadership which comes in time to those who have learned the lessons of reflex obedience and unquestioning followership.

While reflex obedience may be seen as an asset, and a dream scenario for the beleaguered teacher, it both models and reproduces a particular view of what leadership is. It sees leadership and followership in unambiguous interrelationship to one another. Followership, in this simple-minded model, is bought at the price of sacrificing the individual to a greater good, while the 'natural leaders' emerge because they are the resilient survivors. The model carries within it the unintended consequence of disabling the organisation as a whole. This happens because the process, by design or default, diminishes both individual and organisational intelligence, as demonstrated in the words 'Who asked you to think, Private? Thinking is injurious to your health.' This has the effect, in a very literal sense, of shutting down the neurological circuitry in the brain. Multiplied from recruit to recruit, it not only reduces their collective intelligence, but systematically reduces the IQ of the organisation as a whole. 'Well *don't* think, then!', is a line that has, unfortunately, been uttered by many teachers over the decades.

This belief in the value of reflex followership, of systemic built-in learning disabilities, has brought in its wake a harrowing history of human misery and disaster. Paschendale is simply one episode in a shameful catalogue of military incompetence – hundreds of thousands of allied soldiers sent to their deaths by generals poring over maps, far removed from the front line.

In her best-selling book *Longitude* Dava Sobel (1997) tells the story of the ship *The Association*, which foundered on the pinnacle rocks around the Scilly Isles because the captain, outraged by the intelligence of a junior seaman who warned of the imminent danger, had him immediately hanged from the yardarm. Two other ships, *The Eagle* and *The Romney*, followed *The Association* to their own destruction. As Dava Sobel tells it:

> *Such subversive navigation by an inferior was forbidden in the Royal Navy, as the unnamed seaman well knew. However, the danger seemed so enormous by his calculation, that he risked his neck to make his concerns known to the officers. Admiral Shovell had the man hanged for mutiny on the spot. (p. 9)*

This story, told before the discovery of longitude, has a frightening contemporary parallel. The modern version is the *Challenger*. The launch of the *Challenger* spacecraft was on an unusually cold day for Florida. Two technicians were concerned that the unexpected cold might have a deleterious effect on the rubber seals of the spacecraft, and tried to voice their concern to a management that was unable to listen or learn from members so low in the hierarchy. The first and only teacher in space was to be a victim of NASA's learning disability.

A similar frightening tale is told by Daniel Goleman (1996) in his book *Emotional Intelligence*. It recounts the story of McBroom, the airline pilot who exerted such a fearful authority that his co-pilots were too scared to tell him that he was on course for disaster. The result was that the plane crashed, killing ten people because, in Goleman's words, 'his crew co-pilots were so fearful of McBroom's wrath that they said nothing, even as disaster loomed' (p. 148).

These dramatic episodes are examples of failure in true leadership. They may seem, on the face of it, to have little application in the context of schools, but on a more modest scale schools also repeat and relive their mistakes from generation to generation. Schools too may be guilty of failing to learn from their most junior members, from young teachers, from pupils, from support staff, parents or even casual visitors.

In Peter Senge's (1992) list of organisational learning disabilities the first is this – 'I am my position.' In other words, 'The value and weight of what I say is commensurate with my organisational status.' 'I am the headteacher', 'I am the school-keeper' or 'I am chair of the board of governors.' It impels us to ask in our own context – 'To what extent in our school do we filter our corporate "intelligence" through the prism of status?' What does the head say and how is it said? How does management see it? What is the authority's stance? What is the departmental view? The potential disabling lies in testing the value of an idea or practice by the institutional level at which it is endorsed. There is an important discovery to be made – that when people are freed from those hierarchical constraints and enabled to leave position behind them, new possibilities and insights open up and leadership is allowed to emerge in the most unexpected of places.

'Nothing fails like success' is another in Senge's canon of disabilities. In the hierarchical organisation in which status is all, junior staff must, like that all-too-prescient seaman of *The Association*, learn quickly and not be too conspicuously successful because it will be seen as undermining authority. It may risk tarnishing the gloss of those who have a need to occupy centre stage.

This is in the very nature of hierarchy. It is, of course, not always that brutal, cynical or self-serving. It can be benevolent. It can be comfortable and reassuring, but only through the most scrupulous of efforts can it avoid the divisiveness and disabling of its members. That has been the goal pursued by the most visionary heads and reformers who have battled for decades to liberate staff and students through learning-focused leadership. The onus is directly on those who, by virtue of policy and history, are pushed to occupy centre stage, to expose the disabilities of the organisation and help staff, students and parents to recognise and confront them too. A key feature of participative leadership is the capacity to be surprised. As Hampden-Turner and Trompenaars (1993) put it:

> *participation is not a technique designed to get workers to do what their managers wanted in the first place, but a willingness to be surprised by an unforeseen initiative or suggestion. (p. 28)*

The brake of local management

Schools in this brave new world must hereafter manage themselves. The logic of the move to site-based management, as the Americans call it, comes from the international quest for improved quality and competitiveness in world markets. It is driven by economic crises and a culture of accountability and VFM – value for money. Decentralisation and autonomy are government's gift to schools, depicted as thwarted over the years by controlling local bureaucracies. In exchange for this liberation, government's gifts to itself are closer monitoring, evaluation and intervention mechanisms. If schools, along with other public bodies, are to be held to account for their new-found autonomy, it means improved knowledge of performance – of pupils, of teachers and of schools as a whole.

School leaders, located by government policy, at the apex of the organisational pyramid, are expected therefore to be visionary driving forces. This role is graphically depicted in one headteacher's 'self-portrait' as at the wheel of 'the internal combustion engine' impelled by forces largely out of his control (see Figure 2.3). The paradox within the picture is the 'internal' nature of the combustion because, with responsibility devolved to the school, it is the constrictions of its new-found freedoms that fuel the inertia. The devolution of financial accountability to individual school level requires more energy to be invested in the driving, keeping at least one eye on steering the course, leaving less scope for side excursions, interesting detours or exploration of the terrain. There is less opportunity to lead in new directions and more time must be invested in administration. More time must be given to financial management and the political negotiation that comes with the territory.

There is less energy left for cultivating the leadership of others. As Julia Evetts (1994) has argued in her study of secondary heads, when decisions were reached together with the authority, those decisions were based on an accepted consensus of educational needs and priorities. Following devolution

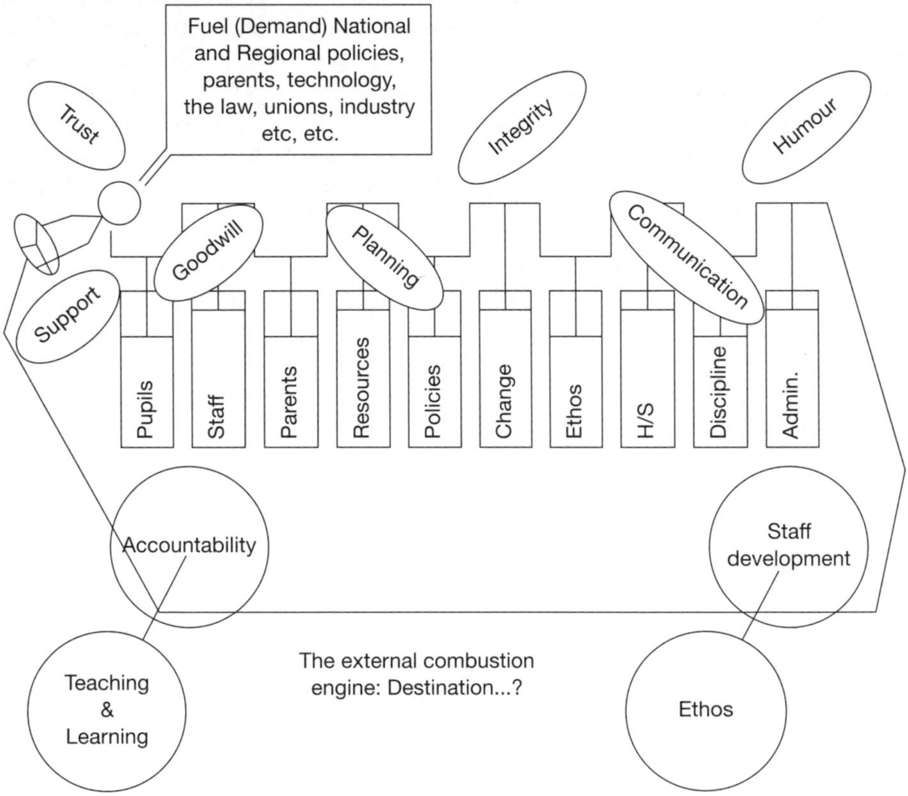

Figure 2.3: The internal combustion engine

to individual schools, however, decisions have tended to be taken more and more on financial and pragmatic grounds and, where once the headteacher negotiated with the authority, the focus of financial bargaining has now turned inwards to the micropolitics of the school.

With local management of schools (LMS) headteachers found that they became involved, and sometimes even obsessed, with things such as furniture and furnishing, heating and lighting, maintenance and repairs, telephone, fax and communication systems, ordering and bookkeeping. For some this proved to be a welcome distraction. For many it was one of the great liberating features of LMS – no more waiting a year for the appropriate authority department to get round to repairs. They were able to circumvent the long delays. Heads could find good deals on the open market, effect instant repairs at minimal cost, install up-to-the-minute communication systems and take advantage of special offers.

However, as the headteachers in Evetts's study discovered, this financial latitude had its downside. Their new-found freedom and flexibility brought with it a tricky juggling of options and priorities. It was no longer a straightforward matter to simply appoint the best person for the job, especially when the school already had a preponderance of staff at the top of the scale. Local management brought with it, too, an increased need to meet with governing bodies. In Evetts's schools, instead of meetings once every six weeks, meetings or sub-committee meetings in some schools became a weekly institution and there was now an increasing pressure on the head and other members of the senior management team to provide information, guidance and direction. Ordering and repairs might have been speeded up but, as the heads in Evetts's study reported, there was an extra burden of bureaucracy and a 'slowing down the whole process of running a school' (Evetts, 1994, p. 112).

There are close echoes of this in a study of Chicago school principals (Bennet *et al.*, 1992). It compared what school principals actually did subsequent to site-based leadership (SBL) and what they believed they should have been doing (illustrated in Figure 2.4).

Site-based leadership had increased the principals' workload and expanded the repertoire of skills they were required to utilise. They were working harder, 60 hours a week or more, but with the feeling that there was never enough time, never enough resources to become effective leaders. Asked to identify roadblocks to exercising the kind of leadership they had envisioned when entering the job, they cited those listed in Figure 2.5.

While some of these are perennial issues of school management, many are either new or come with a new edge and urgency to them. They have close parallels in the United Kingdom. The four roadblocks expressed most often and most strongly by English heads in the Effective Leadership study were very close to those cited by their Chicago counterparts. They had to do with time, funding, professional development and how to deal with inadequate teachers.

Key
a School management
b Central office
c Discipline
d Parents and community
e Student activities
f Instructional leadership
g Professional development

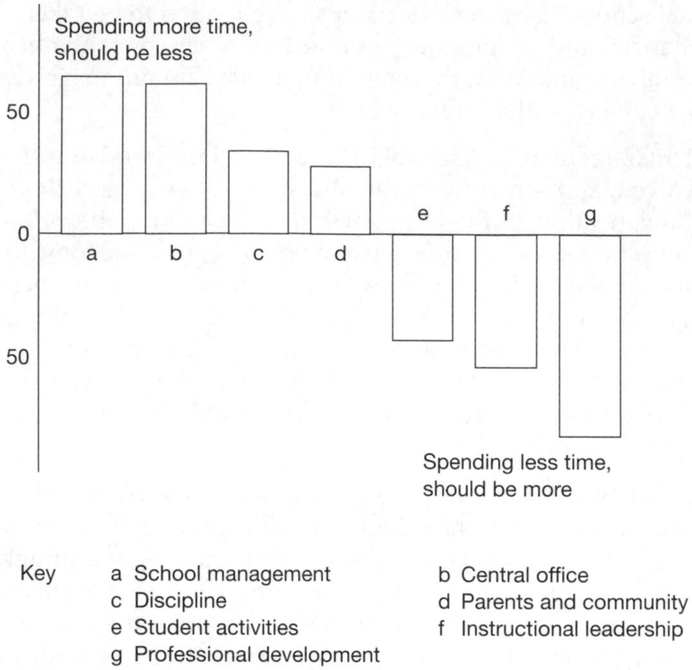

Figure 2.4: The effect of site-based leadership
(*Source*: Bennet *et al.* (1992), p. 25.)

Roadblocks	*% saying 'serious'*
Lack of time for professional development	66
Difficulty of removing poor teachers	65
Time taken for administrative detail at the expense of more important matters	55
Inability to obtain funding	58
Parents apathetic or irresponsible about their children	53
Collective bargaining agreements	54
State or federal mandates	39
Problem students	35
Poor communication from central office	37
Resistance to change from staff	23
Standardised testing practices	26
Lack of recognition/reward for principals	27
Lack of flexibility within the school district	18

Figure 2.5: Roadblocks to leadership
(*Source*: Bennet *et al.* (1992), p. 25.)

Although LMS has been broadly welcomed by headteachers it had, in Evetts's view, changed the nature and orientation of their work. It has had the effect of:

- opening the distance between 'management' and staff;
- increasing the isolation of the head;
- reducing contact with pupils;
- increasing competition;
- requiring greater computer literacy and use of information management systems;
- requiring new skills and frustrating the use of pedagogic skills.

Not all of these are necessarily 'bad' or unwelcome from a head's point of view. Some have enjoyed the reduction of contact with pupils and for some, distance has enhanced their personal status; some thrive on competition. Yet, the effects of this significant change in the context of schools and school leadership have to be clearly understood.

The brake of community capital

'We are being held accountable for the educational capital of the communities in which our schools are located,' said a headteacher whose school was 50th out of 52 in his authority's ranking. He claimed there was a virtually day-to-day pressure on him from the press, a few of the governors, and a handful of parents, to raise standards. He was committed to doing so and had been successful in pushing his school from 52nd to 50th in a year. It was a modest advance but in a context where his competitors were engaged in the same zero-sum game. One of the brakes on his improvement of aggregated attainment data was his special unit for emotionally and behaviourally disturbed children. In addition, there were more than a dozen refugee families newly arrived in the area: some were passing through briefly; others were still to come. The community profile included large numbers of elderly people at one end of the spectrum and a large number of young-parent families at the other. The high rate of pupil absenteeism was, to some degree, explained by responsibilities to the extended family, children looking after sick parents and grandparents or younger siblings. Less than 2 per cent of the adult population in his community had a further, or degree, qualification.

State schools in areas such as his do not have the luxury of choosing their clientele. They must work with those who choose them or increasingly come to them by default, because those parents are less able to exercise choice and their very inability to do so is a salient aspect of the educational capital they bring with them. The rhetoric of choice has to be set against a background of increasing relative poverty and growing disparity in life chances.

Despite a general improvement in living standards, the number of people living in poverty in the UK has increased threefold since 1979 (Mortimore and Whitty, 1999). The proportion of children living in poor households is now 32 per cent compared to the European Union average of 20 per cent. The distance between rich and poor, privileged and underprivileged, has grown progressively during the Thatcher and post-Thatcher years. Mortimore and Whitty conclude:

> *Our country has been exceptional in that the difference between the 'haves' and 'have nots' seems to have resulted from official policies designed to lift the constraints affecting the rich. These policies have sought to penalise the poor in the interest of freeing them from the so-called 'dependency culture'. Britain stands out internationally in having experienced the largest percentage increase in income inequality between 1967 and 1992. (p. 2)*

'It is unethical', says the Canadian researcher Ken Leithwood (1999), 'to hold schools and teachers accountable for things beyond their control.' Raising expectations and standards of achievement is, of course, in part within the compass and power of teachers, and a sharpened sense of accountability is an antidote to unacceptably low expectations and self-fulfiling prophecies. But the famous words of Basil Bernstein (1970) are as relevant now as they were in the 1960s: 'School cannot compensate for society.'

A Spanish observer of the English scene (Tiana *et al.*, forthcoming 1999) commented with some degree of astonishment on the assumption that parental choice of school should, or could, be guided by comparisons of test and examination scores:

> *the only thing taken into consideration are pupils' results in almost exclusively cognitive tests or examinations. The school and even the school management itself run the risk of becoming solely guided with this objective in mind, without really taking into account the complexity and necessary subtlety of implementing change and learning strategies which do not neglect the more formal, personal aspects of the act of learning . . . In view of the fact that, generally speaking, teachers cannot involve themselves to any large extent in systematic curriculum improvements at the national level, the end result is that through intermediate outside institutions the State regains power of control over teachers' instructional activity and in general, over the management and everyday life of schools.*

The double jeopardy is that while diverting teachers from their essential tasks, it is obvious to even the least sophisticated of critics that there are more accurate measures of a community's educational capital than the quality of the school. It is not surprising, then, that of all the brakes on the optimism of leaders for school improvement, it is community capital that is the most challenging, as Micheal Fullan (1997b) explains:

It is easy to be pessimistic about educational reform . . . there have are many legitimate reasons to be discouraged . . . In the same way that crash diets don't work, we must abandon the search for the quick fix. There is a consistent message in the new books on change: have good ideas, but listen with empathy; create time and mechanisms for personal and group reflection; allow intuition and emotion a respected role, work on improving relationships, realise that hope, especially in the face of frustrations, is the last healthy virtue. (p. 14)

It is hope in the face of frustrations that harnesses the energy of the other side of the force field – the accelerators.

The accelerators

Concealed within the negative forces which push against school improvement are the latent positives. Leadership means making the organisation work for you rather than against you, harnessing the negative energy and changing its polarity. It means finding ways of living within the imposed structures, working along the grain in the short term and seeking to break through and transform inhibiting structures in the longer term. The single most powerful asset in this is the school's staff and, however much they may constitute a minority, the committed staff. It is their synergy which can, over time, change the culture.

The accelerator of commitment

The commitment of teachers in the face of adversity is a constant mystery and source of inspiration. How, in the direst of circumstances, in the most heartbreaking of communities and damaged children, do teachers find the energy and good will to persist? Margaret Wheatley (1994) found an answer to this question in demoralised organisations where there 'ought not to have been' commitment or energy, but despite their surroundings people were optimistic and motivated. The secret ingredient was that these people made meaning for themselves:

They were staying creative, making sense out of nonsense, because they'd taken the time to create a meaning for their work – one that transcended present organisational circumstances. They wanted to hold on to motivation and direction in the midst of turbulence, and the only way they could do this was by investing the current situation with meaning. (p. 72).

This is echoed in the findings of two researchers, Hackman and Oldham (1976, p. 157), who identified three conditions which kept people going. They called these:

- 'experienced meaningfulness' – the extent to which a person perceives work as being worthwhile or important, given his or her system of values;
- 'experienced responsibility' – the extent to which a person believes that she or he is personally responsible or accountable for the outcomes of efforts; and
- 'knowledge of results' – the extent to which a person is able to determine on a regular basis whether or not the outcomes of her or his efforts are satisfactory.

The essentially emotional nature of these three conditions is amplified in Andy Hargreaves's (1995) description of what motive power drives good teaching. He says:

> *Good teaching is not just a matter of being efficient, developing competence, mastering technique and possessing the right kind of knowledge. Good teaching also involves emotional work. It is infused with desire, pleasure, mission, creativity, challenge and joy. Good teaching is a profoundly emotional activity. (p. 52).*

Tapping into that reserve of emotional energy is what the prescient leader does as a matter of high priority. She understands that a staff's commitment is enhanced by a sense of professional autonomy and collaboration. Being in control is a basic human need. In his book *The Sickening Mind* Paul Martin (1997) cites biological evidence on the significance of personal control and concludes:

> *It is hardly surprising that our minds – and those of other species – should be so attuned to a sense of personal control, since control over the immediate environment is vital for most organisms' survival. Control signifies autonomy, mastery and empowerment. (p. 145).*

Lack of control induces panic, anxiety, disequilibrium. It is not only those at the apex of the pyramid who need to feel they are in charge. It runs through the whole school from top to bottom. It includes middle management, support staff and teachers. As Willard Waller (1932) wrote more than 60 years ago, the fear of losing control runs like a thread through the whole of a teacher's professional life.

Martin cites evidence to show that:

- control or lack of it is closely related to mental and physical well-being;
- people with less power and control in organisations are more prone to heart disease than people with greater power and control;
- a sense of being in control helps to deal with and lessen stress;
- social support and networking lessens stress and risks of illness.

He goes on to suggest a matrix with two key dimensions – demand and control – see Figure 2.6.

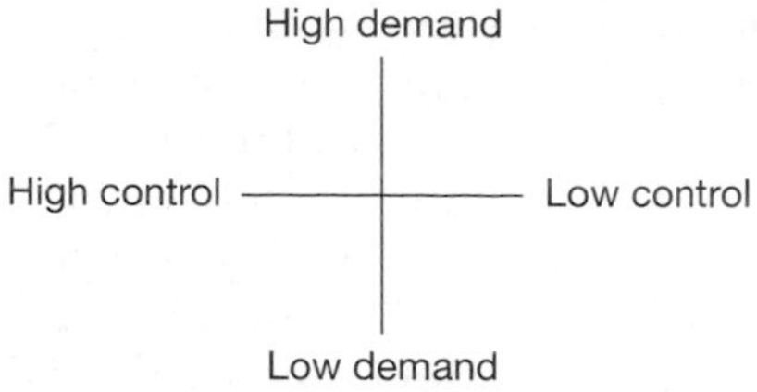

Figure 2.6: Demand and control matrix
(*Source*: Martin (1997))

He demonstrates that the worst situation to be in is high demand/low control. When there is pressure from above, it diminishes performance, exacerbates stress and reduces resistance and immunity, making people more susceptible to illness and disease. On the other hand, as Csikszentmihalyi (1990) has shown in his work on 'flow' – the psychology of optimal experience – a high level of control but little demand leads to apathy and boredom, providing no incentive for improvement.

The paradox for leadership is that, alongside the personal need to be in charge of events, a sense of control is just as vital for the most junior members of the organisation. In some sense, indeed, they need it most. Paradoxically, the headteacher can most easily relinquish control because she will reap the benefits when control is exercised at the lower levels of the organisation. Raising standards and improving schools then come not through 'levering up' or from downward pressure, but from an intrinsically satisfying challenge which engages and enhances the professional skills of the teacher.

This is what Thomas Sergiovanni (1992) describes as 'pedagogical leadership'. He provides a helpful distinction among four aspects of leadership which he terms 'bureaucratic', 'visionary', 'entrepreneurial' and 'pedagogical'. Bureaucratic leadership, he suggests, is characterised by systems which emphasise supervision, evaluation and incentives. Visionary leadership relies on inspiration and 'a powerfully spoken sense of what must be done'. Entrepreneurial leadership, applying market principles, encourages competition, incentives and sanctions for winners and losers. Pedagogical leadership invests in and builds capital. The capital which it builds is the professional and intellectual capacity of teachers. With this a school is in a position to enhance the social and academic capital of its students.

In its popular connotation, 'strong' leadership is unlikely to equate with pedagogical leadership as described by Sergiovanni, yet 'strong' may indeed be the most apt term for it because, among the four types, pedagogical leadership is the one that requires the greatest inner strength and moral integrity. It is not 'strong' as in the exercise of personal or institutional power, but strong in inner conviction that goals will be achieved through strengthening the status and commitment of others, even at the cost of diminishing self.

This is not the image of 'strong' leadership in the popular and political idiom. Its vocabulary is of a quite different register. It does not use the vocabulary of 'driving up' and 'levering up' standards, of the 'push' and 'pressure' and the rationale that where this fails it is due to 'resistance' by teachers and 'obstacles' in the path of government's 'drive'. The lexicon underpinning this model of strong directive leadership is so deeply ingrained and is lent such reinforcement from national policy and popular press that it is hard to resist. 'Pedagogical leadership is a nice idea', said a headteacher in our research study, 'but how can it work in the real and pressured world of schools?' As Simkins *et al.* (1992) points out, in the nineties world of schools, the world of corporate management, control lies firmly at the top:

> *The shift from the sixties/seventies to the eighties/nineties has been away from people-centredness and consensus to competition, personal assertiveness, firm leadership, strong control – the characteristics of corporate managerialism. (p. 120)*

Pedagogical leadership is a riskier business. One headteacher spoke about risk-taking in these terms:

> *It was a gamble I suppose, but I wanted to test the waters, to break the mould of Buggin's turn and the time-server's charter. I appointed an NQT [newly qualified teacher] to chair a working party, in it some senior members of staff and a few old hands – very old hands. But I thought we would all learn something. Even if it seemed like a disaster. I reckoned we had the reserve capacity to cope and to move forward.*

The headteacher who gave responsibility to the youngest teacher in the school to chair a working party knew she was taking a risk, had weighed up the consequences of possible disaster but had carried it through none the less because she saw in it an opportunity for everyone to learn, including herself. It was an opportunity to loosen the grip on the reins of control and allow it to be enjoyed and exercised by others. It was an opportunity to be surprised by what commitment can bring.

Commitment multiplied may be described as 'synergy', the collective force that is greater than the sum of its parts. Warren Bennis (1997), who has examined what he called 'great groups', found that 'people in great groups seem to become better than themselves. They are able to see more, achieve more and have a far better time doing it than they can working alone' (p. 196).

Although the ability to work together towards a shared goal was a prerequisite for membership of a great group, being amiable, or even pleasant, wasn't. Bennis says:

> *Great groups are probably more tolerant of personal idiosyncrasies than ordinary ones, if only because the members are so intensely focused on the work itself. Their all-important task acts as a social lubricant, minimising frictions. Sharing information and advancing the work are the only real social obligations. (p. 203)*

While Bennis is referring here to high-powered groups such as those engaged in the Manhattan Project, it is a thought-provoking conclusion when applied in an educational context. Probably everyone can remember, from their own school experience, teachers who were idiosyncratic to the point of eccentricity and neither 'pleasant' nor 'amiable' in any conventional sense, but who had a passion for their subject and for their pupils. Contemporary schools appear much less diverse and tolerant of idiosyncrasy and senior management teams tend increasingly towards the managerialist executive image.

People who are engaged in ground-breaking collaborations, concludes Bennis, 'have high regard for people who challenge and test their ideas' (p. 203). While great groups have their own individual leaders, these leaders are *primus inter pares*. The emergent leader in a great group is described by Bennis as a 'curator'. Their job is not to make, but to choose. They have insights into where to go to find answers and who to choose for a job. Like conductors, they may not be able to play the instrument, but they have an understanding of the qualities that it should produce. James Dyson, whose name has been lent to a household product just as Hoover's was before him, argues that advances in engineering are not always made by engineers and that inventions are frequently the product of people working outside that particular field. They dare to ask the naïve questions which no one has asked before, and in so doing shake and change the very foundations of the enterprise.

Commitment is an accelerator and increases velocity to the extent that opportunities are created for people to form coalitions, to lead and to challenge, to exceed their own boundaries and expectations. A strategic procedure for a school's management team is what one research team has called 'appreciative inquiry' (Cooperrider and Srivasta, 1999). It builds on and multiplies energy and proceeds in four stages:

1. appreciate the best of what is
2. ask what it could be like if you could only have more of the good things identified
3. encourage discourse in order to find out what it should be like
4. decide what it will be like.

The accelerator of professional learning

Commitment to the school, to the job, to colleagues and to pupils generally carries with it a commitment to professional development. In turn this implies confronting the disabilities of the organisation and identifying what we might call the learning *ability* of the school. This is a form of appreciative inquiry. In order to do this we need to apply what we know about how individuals learn and how they overcome blocks and barriers to learning. There are some things we can say with confidence about this process, based on the best evidence from psychology, neuroscience and educational research. People learn when there is:

- a reason or a stimulus to learn
- a climate which encourages exploration and risk-taking
- models to observe and learn from
- opportunities to test out what is being learned
- the possibility of success
- opportunities to learn from mistakes
- support and encouragement
- feedback about success and progress
- self-belief
- an audience to share in the benefits of learning.

Applying these as a set of criteria by which to examine the school as an organisation suggests that some criteria are easier to meet than others. We might test these as seen through the eyes of the newly qualified teacher who comes with fresh insights and is keen to know what kind of school this is. She may ask: 'Is it one that will recognise the knowledge and expertise that I already possess? Will it value the peculiar assets and talents I bring with me? Will it appreciate the optimism and expectation that has brought me to make this commitment? Will it make allowances for my self-doubt and allow me to take risks and to fail sometimes, as well as providing the best conditions for success? Will it offer me the opportunity to share openly with others what I have done well and feel free to admit to private disasters? Will I have the occasion to learn from others and will others be "big" enough to learn from me? Is this a school in which people talk about learning and on a daily basis ask of themselves as well as of their pupils, "What did you learn in school today?".'

There are many countries in which most of these criteria could not be met. Teachers have their own classrooms and their own classes, and they teach unobserved by other adults, sometimes for the length of their professional career. As 'qualified' teachers, well versed in their subject, there is no impetus to learn more, no corporate ethos to encourage it, no feedback, and no wider audience than the cohorts of pupils who pass through from year to year. This was the character of many schools in Britain within the recent past, and many schools still retain some of those characteristics.

In a world that is changing so rapidly, however, the nature of professional knowledge is being challenged and needs to be continuously recreated. The teacher of French language may have comparatively little still to learn about her discipline, but will forever have to wrestle with the problem of how to share her knowledge with all her pupils. The older she gets the more distanced she will become from the life experiences of those she teaches and, without strenuous and sensitive effort, less able to tune into and empathise with their situation. She may have a high level of expertise in the methodology of teaching French to children, but find it difficult to help a newly qualified teacher do what she does so effortlessly. She may do many things well but lack the vocabulary and conceptual insight to explain it to others, to her colleagues, to parents. She may have little idea of how to advise a parent on how to support their child through difficulties and low self-confidence. She may see no reason to share her knowledge with the teacher of Physics, to observe a lesson in Home Economics or to learn from the teacher of Mathematics.

Argyris and Schön (1978) write about 'self-sealing' systems. These are organisations that do not know how to progress and improve. They have no mechanisms or tools to confront their own practices and to create their own intelligence.

Salomon and Perkins (1998) describe 'self-sealing systems' in a school context where school leaders and teachers 'pursue agendas while concealing them', and in which 'individuals aim unilaterally to protect both themselves and others against the stress of negative feedback'. Breaking the seal means engaging in 'double-loop learning'. The first stage is 'single-loop learning', providing feedback so that people can become aware of, and change, their behaviour. The second stage, the second loop, is where people reflect on that single-loop process and share it with others. In Salomon and Perkins's words:

> *This involves helping individuals to air and test their tacit assumptions publicly, avoid unilateral protection of themselves or others, and come together in collective problem-solving process that deals with large-scale tacit issues, not just surface technical issues. (p. 15)*

Making knowledge for yourself, as a group of staff, is the most exhilarating impetus that a school can enjoy. This happens, says David Hargreaves (1999), when school leaders work forward 'with the grain' of teachers' experience and motivation. He uses a horticultural metaphor ('beloved of educationists since Plato') to describe the process through which teachers create knowledge for themselves. The five stages are sowing, germinating, thinning, shaping and pruning, and showing and exchanging. This casts the headteacher in the role of estate manager, whose primary task is to maintain the climate for growth and tend to the process of cross-pollination.

The first stage is the sowing of ideas. Teachers possess an immense repertoire of tacit knowledge which is expressed in what they do spontaneously, naturally, intuitively, but is inaccessible to others until it can be transformed into explicit knowledge. The 'seeding' is the collegial dialogue and networking, but in order for germination to take place incipient growth needs to be guarded and protected. Good ideas – especially when they come from new or more junior colleagues – are fragile and may well need protection by the most experienced teachers from colleagues inclined to intellectual infanticide. 'Cynics kill knowledge creation', says Hargreaves. Thinning means ensuring that growth is not choked by so wild a proliferation of ideas that the good and the best are not given the space to flourish. Shaping and pruning is the stage of validation of new knowledge, testing its resilience and its capacity as a new and viable strain. The self-conscious attempt to validate practice requires opportunities for teachers to both watch one another at work and develop a conceptual frame for talking principles-in-practice. The 'third eye' of critical friend or inspector may well be necessary to add the critical edge to what is seen and how it is judged. So, the final stage in the horticultural sequence, 'showing', takes place with a high degree of confidence that the practice is open to scrutiny and amenable to wider distribution.

Hargreaves's extended metaphor does, however, lack one essential ingredient, that is, 'grafting'. It is through grafting that new strains are created, frequently with unexpected consequences. Ultimately it is probably grafting that will allow the kind of divergent growth that underwrites the school's future.

In the Hargreaves model the role of the leadership is more implicit than explicit but it presupposes a high level of gardening skills – a deep knowledge, a light touch, a passion for growth. Such passion in the horticultural model is about tending to the growth of others. To do this successfully, as the gardening metaphor suggests, means being one step ahead in anticipation and planning, but constantly open to surprise and new insights.

The accelerator of parental partnership

A school may see its primary task as reaching out to its community to play a part in enriching its educational life and working with other agencies towards a more civilised future for its children. In our experience, young teachers often find teaching most challenging and rewarding in areas of economic disadvantage because they can see that they make a difference. The most rewarding aspect of a teacher's job is to see evidence of children and young people's growth as individuals, as social and emotional beings infused with self-belief and with a commitment to learning.

In challenging areas good teachers find it profoundly satisfying to work with the community, helping to rebuild a trust in the world and shoring up fragile self-esteem. When required to sacrifice this often slow and long-term goal for pragmatic, short-term, and competitive gains, however, they become rapidly disillusioned. In a recent survey for the National Union of Teachers, Galton and Fogelman (1997) found that there had been, in recent years, a narrowing and limiting of opportunities for 'spontaneous encounters' and loss of those 'magic moments' which made teaching enjoyable and rewarding. They concluded, 'Such encounters help forge the excellent teacher–pupil relationships on which effective learning must be based.' They might have added to that the equally significant home–school relationship within which effective learning is seeded and nurtured.

The Canadian researcher Peter Coleman (1998) describes this fertile groundbed of learning as 'the power of three'. Figure 2.7 illustrates a number of different versions of this triadic relationship. The first, represented diagrammatically by three pluses, is the relationship most likely to produce high achievement. As we have learned from Reuven Feuerstein *et al.*'s (1980) work, the difference between success and failure is less explained by what happens in schools and classrooms than by what happens beyond the school gates. Nor, as Feuerstein *et al.* demonstrate, is the determining factor poverty, parental education or income. The key issue is how learning is mediated by adults or older siblings.

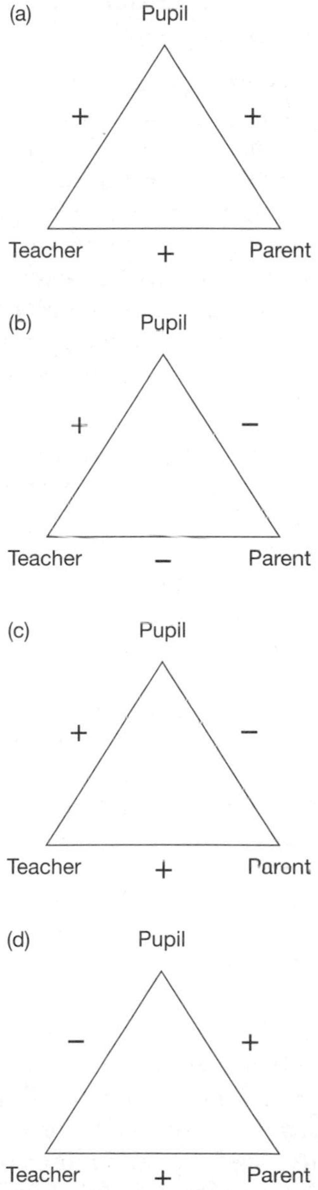

(a) The ideal, where learning is built on educative relationships among parents, teachers and pupils working to common goals.

(b) There is a positive learning–teaching relationship in the classroom but this cannot compensate for the lack of educative relationship in the home or between teacher and parent.

(c) There is a strong teaching–learning relationship in the classroom and a supportive parent relationship. The parent needs support and help to deal with the negative relationship with the pupil.

(d) The positive relationship between parent and child and between parent and teacher cannot compensate for the negative teacher–pupil relationship. There is enough positive energy to find a solution, but the onus is primarily on the school to find that solution.

Figure 2.7: Versions of the triadic relationship

Parents or other adults help to structure meaning for children in the critical years when they are building their neural networks and developing theories about themselves and about the nature of the world. Emotionally secure, self-confident adults can give that quality of support to their offspring and shepherd them through the challenges of childhood, encouraging them to face and overcome those challenges for themselves, knowing there is a secure supporting hand behind them. Where this occurs it is a priceless gift for the teacher, who can not only build on these well-laid foundations, but knows that she can go on building successfully in concert with a concerned parent.

In the second example (Figure 2.7 (b)) the teacher–pupil relationship is the only strength (one plus as against two minuses). Where this is the case there is a constant uphill struggle, one that is highly inimical to success unless strategies can be found to work with the other two sides of the relationship. Family-centred learning and projects which bring parent, teacher and child together, either in a school or home setting, are examples of how this can be tackled. These strategies may also be used where school and home (or teacher and parent) forge a positive relationship but the parent–child relationship is problematic (Figure 2.7 (c)). Inter-agency work, or parental workshops that help parents rebuild their relationships with their children are ways in which this has been tackled.

The fourth example (Figure 2.7 (d)), where the teacher–pupil relationship is weak but the other relationships are strong, is the one in which both the problem and the solution rest more with the school and school leadership than in the home or in the home–school interface. In this area the school's, and the leadership's, accountability is most clear-cut. Reorganising classes and timetabling may be one solution; team teaching and changing of roles another. Changing the context of the relationship through extra-curricular activities, residential experience or after-school study support have been shown, in many instances, to effect a significant change in the relationship. Very often it is not the pupil who has to do the adjustment but the teacher, who not only begins to see the pupil in a new light but come to a new understanding of learning and the learning relationship. Parent involvement in study support is a plus, but more valuable in some cases than others.

In all of these initiatives schools have a role to play. In addressing this sensitive but immensely significant issue it is helpful to be reminded of the very different contexts in which children and young people are required to pursue their learning. Peter Hannon (1993) makes the distinctions between school and home learning shown in Figure 2.8.

The *Home from School* (MacBeath *et al.*, 1986) research study found that schools could often provide a richness, flexibility and closeness of relationships and conversation not to be found in the home. In some cases the home environment, or even the child's own private world, was fuller and more complex than the threadbare learning offered in their classrooms. In other cases still

School learning	*Home learning*
• shaped by curriculum • bounded by sanctions • timetabled • contrived problems • restricted language • limited conversations • special resources – limited access • recognition of achievement in approved areas • horizontal age group • distant relationship with adults • pupil role • accounts for little variation in academic achievement	• shaped by interest • spontaneous • flexible • natural problems • everyday language • extended conversations • 'natural' resources – unlimited access • recognition of achievement in many areas • vertical age group • close relationship with adults • multiple roles • accounts for much variation in academic achievement

Figure 2.8: Distinctions between school and home learning

there was a similar depth, or shallowness, of experience in both school and out-of-school contexts. In relation to the experience of young children, Peter Hannon (1993) has argued that parents can be, in some important respects, more effective teachers of reading than school teachers. He concluded from his own research that:

- pre-school teachers seriously underestimated the value of parental support for children's reading;
- the quality of children's experiences in reading to their parents was in some respects superior to what happened in school;
- home readings were longer and had fewer interruptions than reading sessions in the classroom;
- parents' relationship with children allowed them to relate what they were reading to children's experience;
- teachers used praise more, but it was often a mechanism of control and a reflection of their more distant relationship with the child.

In the *Home from School* study it was the first-hand experience of extended conversations with children and their parents in their own natural surroundings that emphasised to the researchers the differential quality of classroom and home, and the immense complexity of the interrelationship of these two sites for learning and socialisation. Schools that asked young people at different stages to keep a detailed log for one week, documenting what they did, who with, and how long they spent on it, were surprised and at first disbelieving about what young people did in trying to manage learning for themselves away from the pressures of the classroom. There were some who had private tutors in a range of school subjects and, at the other extreme, young people who, left entirely to their own devices, invested huge amounts of time on ineffective, unfocused copying or reading, struggling to make their own sense of the printed page or giving up at the first hurdle. Some had the physical and psychological space, encouragement and support from parents or peers who knew little about the subject-matter but had a lot of good sense about timing and pacing and strategies for finding out. Some lived in conditions which crowded out all possibilities for school-related learning.

Teachers involved in that study confessed to knowing very little about the context for children's learning out of school and gained a great deal from the log-keeping exercise. Very often the pupil logs and follow-up exploration of these individually and in groups revealed an underlying failure on the part of the school to think through the relationship of in-school to out-of-school learning. While learning *in* school had in some primary schools become more varied, more differentiated and more imaginative, learning *out* of school seemed to be stuck in a time warp. Classroom learning was often stimulating and inventive; pupils worked in pairs and groups and discussed and shared what they were doing. In the evening, work at home was, as one boy put it, 'a lonely and tedious activity'. Homework tasks were not given the same thought as to the needs of the learner, nor to the coherence and progression of learning.

Advice to young people and their parents often betrayed a lack of understanding of the character of children's learning out of school, for example advocating a quiet place to work, a desk and a desk light, an upright chair, a place free from interruptions. Young people were encouraged to plan their time over the week, by means of a timetable for a routine of work in the early evening or after school. These failed to reflect the reality of young people's lives. Like adults, they worked in a variety of ways and places and at times which suited their domestic routines or personal biorhythms, or fitted the ecology and social composition of the home.

Children and young people need a high level of support to move between these two contexts, and few schools are really good at building effective bridges between home learning and school learning. But it is a growing priority and with it there is growing a body of good practice. Wilhite and Basnet (1999) conclude:

> *Making learning that happens outside the classroom more intentional doesn't really require great changes in the way we teach. It requires only a change in the way we think about teaching and learning and about who is responsible for it. (p. 2)*

The most challenging question for leadership – individual and collective – is 'Who is responsible for learning in the school?'

In conclusion

Good leadership means putting the organisation to work. The first step is to be aware of the nature of the organisation that, as a headteacher, one is required to lead. The second step is to share that awareness among all stakeholders. They need to see and understand how organisations can inhibit the wider development of initiative and shared leadership and how schools can so easily become disabled by their very own structures. Identifying the brakes and accelerators is one practical way forward. Through appreciative inquiry the school can engage in the progressive removal of barriers to a wider and more profound meaning of leadership.

Appendix 2.1
Seven steps to the learning school

The following may be seen as stages, pursued in sequence, or as key constituent parts which come together over time to form a coherent whole.

1 **Promote a learning climate**: The school leadership models learning in action. Instead of MBWA (management by walking about) they exemplify LBWA (learning by walking about), using opportunities to tune into what Jennifer Nias (1989) calls 'the secret harmonies' of the school. Talking and reading about learning is encouraged. Seminal education research publications are available and referred to.

2 **Identify the green shoots of growth**: Where in the school are the exemplary learners – not necessarily the very best teachers but those who are most open and keen to learn and to share? Who are the best listeners? Who encourage feedback from their pupils? Who talk about learning in the staffroom? Who seek out alliances with other teachers across disciplines? Which members of staff use positive language? Who are the energy creators? 'Appreciative inquiry' is the name given to this process.

3 **Identify the barriers:** Improvement is less likely to be helped by innovation than by removing the blocks and barriers to learning. Where is the energy and intelligence of the school being drained off? What and who are the high energy consumers? Where does the cynicism creep in? What practices and protocols have never been challenged?

4 **Share pedagogical leadership:** Provide opportunities for exemplary learners to exercise leadership. Offer opportunities for newly qualified teachers to lead groups and build teams. Involve pupils in feedback and decisions about learning and teaching, and give them a role in consultative and policy-making groups.

▶

5 **Create intelligence from within:** Make learning the central focus and business of the school. Encourage the belief that knowledge can be found as much within the school as from external sources. Build alliances and networks of learners. Provide time and support for the networkers. Challenge people to move beyond their comfort zone.

6 **Use critical friends:** Engage one or more outside 'experts' to work with staff as a friend of the schools but ensure that they are people with not only the skills to listen sensitively and support good practice but the skills and courage to challenge and to draw theory out of tacit knowledge. Consider other critical friends internal to the school who might also play that role for their colleagues.

7 **Build resilient networks:** Seek out allies from whom you can learn and who are equally open to learning from you. They may be local or they may be in another country. Internet and European projects have made inter-country exchanges (of personnel, ideas, good practice) more feasible. Practices do not always transplant easily into new soil, but if the underpinning principles are sound they can be adapted and grafted to thrive in another climate.

3

■ ■ ■

Talking Heads

How and why do teachers become headteachers? What motivates and inspires them? What are their primary sources of satisfaction in the job and what do they find the least satisfying aspects? What competencies do they bring and what competences are expected of them from those they are expected to serve? And why did they come to enter teaching in the first place?

These were some of the questions addressed to headteachers in a series of interviews published in the *Times Educational Supplement* under the generic title 'Talking Heads' (Myers, 1995–1998). It involved 27 teachers from nursery, primary, special and secondary schools, 20 of them from British schools, 2 from Canada, 2 from the USA and 1 each from New Zealand, Australia and South Africa. This was not a 'scientific' selection of heads. What they had in common was that somebody, somewhere, had recommended them as a 'good' head and as someone who would be interesting to interview. In this chapter we try to draw together some of the common and disparate strands from those interviews. They illustrate the importance of context, of leadership style, of stages in career progression, and highlight some of the differences between experiences of a first and a second headship.

Why did they enter teaching in the first place?

When asked why they had become teachers the heads divided themselves into three distinct groups:

- The Drifters
- The Late Starters
- The Determined.

Of those 27 heads interviewed, eight had not consciously chosen teaching as a career but had entered the profession through sheer accident and/or serendipitous events. For The Drifters, teaching had not been part of any original game plan. They came into teaching due to lack of career advice; unwillingness to go straight to work after graduating; lack of any clear alternative options; or because their university subject led them nowhere else but into teaching. Some had enjoyed the experience of temporary teaching jobs and then decided to go to college or university to qualify as teachers.

> *After I'd graduated from high school, I travelled through South America and went to visit my sister in Ecuador. She was teaching and I applied for a temporary job in the same school. I thought they'd give me a crash course in teaching but I just got a set of books and was left to swim or sink. I liked it so much that I decided to come home and get a degree in elementary education at the university of New Mexico.*
> *(Male primary head, USA)*

Some of the heads interviewed started out in other careers but found the work environment of the bank, the treasury department or the office uncongenial and discovered what they had been looking for in teaching.

> *I left school at 16 and worked in a bank for two years but did not really like the office environment. I went to speak to one of my old teachers, a nun, who advised me that teaching might be what I was looking for. (Female primary head, England)*

Being 'surprised', 'enthused' or 'inspired' by their first experience of teaching had, for some, kindled the 'flame' which had been burning below the level of consciousness:

> *When I left school I worked for a year as a technical surveyor and became interested in photogrammetry. However, because of apartheid I was told that there was no future in that field for me and so I had to rethink my life. I spoke with an English woman who had been my biology teacher and she suggested teaching. She kindled a flame that had probably been burning all the time. (Male primary head, South Africa)*

The phenomena of drifting into the profession has been noted elsewhere, for example in Julia Evetts's work. It has significant implications for recruitment and teacher supply, making prediction difficult and undermining rational planning. It is difficult to influence and control the flow when, for a significant number, deciding to become a teacher has more to do with chance and circumstance than any overt rational career plan.

The next group, The Late Starters, consisted mainly but not entirely of women, at least two of whom started teaching because of a connection with the school that their own children attended. It was the example of individual teachers that had enthused them and, as one of the interviewees said, it was the way in which primary teachers seemed to be 'thinking about the nature of learning' that had ignited her interest.

> *I had three babies close together so took up part-time work in FE. As my own children started school I started to realise how important primary education is and I was very impressed by the way primary teachers seemed to be thinking about the*

nature of learning. One day when I took my youngest child to school, I was asked if I was a teacher and if I'd be interested in applying for a part-time remedial reading job. I did, got the job, gradually increased my time until I was a class teacher and then a language post holder. I learned on the job like an apprentice, watching what other people were doing. (Female primary head, England)

The final group, The Determined, had known from a very young age exactly what they wanted to do. They had not so much 'drifted' into teaching as moved almost seamlessly into the profession because their parents were teachers; because they had 'played school' when they were young; because the profession was a respectable one to enter; or because they been brought up in an environment which made them inclined to see teaching as a natural progression.

I always wanted to be a teacher. When I was young, being a teacher was very respectable here in my community and I grew up playing school. (Female secondary head, USA)

I always wanted to be a teacher partly because my mother was one. (Female primary head, England)

Some heads spoke about specific events, 'moments of truth' that set them on a course into teaching. The unique and idiosyncratic nature of these key moments is illustrated in the following description from a Scottish primary head teacher:

I wanted to be a teacher from the time in primary school that I sprained my wrist, and because I couldn't write the teacher allowed me to read for three days which were the most wonderful three days of my life. I decided I wanted to teach so that everyone could read. I then remember going to see Mrs McOuat, the head, to ask her something and found her sitting in front of the fire in her office reading the paper. Although she spent a long time trying to convince me that she'd been in school since very early that morning and that this was the first time she had sat down, I still thought that this must be a wonderful way to spend your time. (Male primary head, Scotland)

Satisfaction in teaching was not felt because it was seen as an easier, more comfortable life, but, for several of the heads, because it was challenging.

I started teaching ROSLA (Raising of the School Leaving Age) . . . in a school that was under siege. The staffroom was regularly boarded up after thefts. There were about twenty probationary teachers and we gave each other a great deal of support. After three years I became a year tutor and did that for five years, then moved on to a larger school as head of year. I loved it and stayed for six years before becoming pastoral deputy and then curriculum deputy at another . . . school. (Female secondary head, England)

I worked with juvenile delinquents, including murderers and rapists and was at the same school for 14 years – probably too long. ... It was a great place to work. (Male secondary head, Canada)

For people outside the profession it might seem a surprising conclusion that such a school could be 'a great place to work', but the challenge, collegial support, the knowledge that the work was valued and the recognition that this was something that you could do well, had been a major factor in these people staying in teaching and moving on eventually to become headteachers.

Many of the heads interviewed recognised from an early point in their teaching careers that they were good at what they did:

> *I was a successful teacher and loved children. (Male primary head, USA)*

Not all were quite so confident. One Asian primary head described her own uncertainty:

> *I was very happy at the school, I loved teaching and stayed for ten years . . . The [next] school was involved in an HMI exercise and I was observed teaching by four different inspectors at the same time. I was sure that I must be doing something terribly wrong and that I was going to get into trouble but it turned out that they were very impressed with what they saw. (Female primary head, England)*

Becoming a head

The interviewees' answers to why they had become heads divided them into four different groups:

- The Inadvertent
- The Premeditated
- The Strategists
- The Civic Servants.

Very few of the heads had thought about headship at the beginning of their careers and had described themselves as having 'no clear ambition'; they did not see themselves as heads even 'in their imagination'. They seemed to get there *inadvertently*.

> *I did not map it out when I started. I've always done the next job that presents itself. (Female primary head, England)*

> *It was accidental . . . I tend to jump and see what it's like when I get there. (Male primary head, England)*

> *I never set out to be principal. (Female secondary head, Australia)*

> *The only active career move I made was moving from being a pastoral head to becoming a deputy. (Female secondary head, England)*

Many of them just climbed the next step up the promotion ladder without any particular career plan and only knew they wanted to become heads when they had reached the level of deputy. It was not before this stage that the possibility of headship emerged. This is not surprising for those for whom there had been no role model to follow.

> *I had no clear ambition to be a head. When I started teaching I had no role models; the concept of a female headteacher in mixed secondary schools did not exist. (Female secondary head, Scotland)*

The next group knew as soon as they started teaching that they wanted to become heads. For The Premeditated there were no doubts about this career objective.

> *Once I became a teacher I knew I wanted to be a head. (Female primary head, Scotland)*

> *I did not always want to be a teacher, but once I became one I always wanted to become a head. (Male secondary head, Wales)*

> *Once I started teaching, I wanted to become a head because of the inspirational heads I worked with. (Male primary head, Scotland)*

The third group, The Strategists, decided they wanted to be heads when they realised that this was the only way to get things done.

> *When I started I knew I wanted to influence what happened which meant becoming a head. (Male primary head, England)*

Impatience to 'make things happen' had motivated some to move from the classroom to the larger stage of school management. They wanted to 'influence what happened', which meant having the power and authority to effect it. There was a tension here, though, for those who got a lot of satisfaction from the classroom.

> *I wanted to stay in the classroom but I also wanted to make things happen. (Female primary head, England)*

The members of the final group, The Civic Servants, were both from the USA. These two very different heads (one Hispanic male primary, from Albuquerque; the other black American, female secondary from Memphis) both described their desire to make things happen in terms of civic responsibility, of 'giving something back'.

> *This is the community I grew up in and it has now become virtually abandoned leaving the poorest of poor families. I thought it was time to give something back. (Female secondary head, USA)*

> *I believe that good people have a civic responsibility to step forward and apply for leadership positions, whatever arena it is. (Male primary head, USA)*

These American heads spoke without reservation or embarrassment about 'service' and, although they may well have felt a similar mission, none of the British headteachers spoke in this way. This might be explained by a culture which discourages such overt discussion of community service, or perhaps it can ascribed to the Thatcherite and post-Thatcherite ethos of self-interest, managerialism and 'me firstism'. It may also be due to a perception of teachers and heads that their value has been diminished and their work undermined by successive governments and popular media. In this context the feeling of belonging to a 'noble profession' perhaps seemed less appropriate, while the notion of contributing to the 'public good' did not sit easily with the current recruitment crisis and performance-related pay.

Living up to expectations

Becoming a head involved not only a shift in role, but also a change in status and relationships. The biggest surprise for many of these heads was the way in which they were now perceived by others. While they saw themselves as 'the same person with the same feelings and emotions; others responded to them with a new deference and distance, investing them with authority and omniscience – as one primary head put it, 'thinking you can resolve the problems of the universe':

> *I could not believe the deference and how important people thought you were just because you were principal. It astounded me . . . as a principal you must never underestimate the impact you have. (Male secondary head, Canada)*

> *what I hadn't fully appreciated was the business of being perceived as an all-powerful figurehead. Wherever you are in the school people are checking you out and your words have a significance – if you don't smile people wonder if there's a reason. I've stopped making throw-away jokes because all sorts of things get read into them. People treat you differently even from when you're a deputy. (Female secondary head, England)*

As one primary head said, it was a surprise not to be treated any longer as a colleague but suddenly 'to be taken so seriously'. In the words of a secondary head, 'People put great store by what you say'.

The next big surprise for heads was the reality of being 'in charge' and 'in control'. The 'buck stopping here' came as a shock to some of them, who described this aspect as 'intimidating' and 'daunting'.

> *I was very daunted initially though they probably did not realise it. At first I also found it difficult to cope with the fact that there was no one after me – I was in charge. (Female primary head, England)*

> *Everything [was different than expected]. There was no one to ask what to do or to turn to when I had a problem. Everyone expected me to be in control all the time. It is having to manage everyone else and no one to manage you but yourself. (Female primary head, England)*

I'd had experience of being an acting head but even so the most shocking thing when I first came here was that people expected me to know things. (Male secondary head, England)

Trying to live up to the expectations of a range of different audiences, and trying to 'please everyone by being nice' were unexpected traps. Some heads were unprepared for the number of hats they were required to wear, 'from social worker to financial whiz kid', and the multiple sources of pressure from staff, students, parents, the education authority, DfEE, OFSTED, the public generally and local and national politicians. One head commented that managing adults was more difficult and complicated than managing children.

Several were surprised at how long real, embedded change took.

Understanding that change cannot happen overnight; it is a longer, slower and ongoing process. The realisation of the constraints that heads work under and the various audiences that have to be addressed and whose interests need to be managed. You cannot go on a training course for that, the skill has to evolve and develop – be honed on the job. Although I have been a head for eleven years, I'm still learning. When I stop is the day to pack it up. (Female secondary head, Scotland)

'To build up a good school takes a long time', said one primary head; the amount to learn was greater and 'the picture was much bigger' than anything that had gone before.

At first there were lots of headaches and heartaches. I was not au fait with the system things like legal every day requirements, staffing, ratios, funding. I was so green. It was a crash course in learning! (Female head all-age school, New Zealand)

Some of the interviewees had underestimated the resistance to change and others' belief that staff would want to play a larger role in decision-making had met with the disappointing realisation that democracy takes longer. There was a somewhat poignant comment from the South African head:

I thought that teachers would welcome playing a role in running their school. I think I underestimated the legacy of apartheid that enslaved so many of us. I thought that with democracy everything would become much easier but it will take time – for example for teachers to become affirmed in meetings. (Male primary head, South Africa)

The second-timers

Three of the heads interviewed were on their second headship and had all noted differences between their first and second experiences of headship.

The main difference is that the second time you know what you want and are far more confident about it. In your first headship you grow into the job and become a head. In your second headship you arrive as a head. (Male secondary head, Wales)

There are strong parallels with the Effective Leadership study in which head teachers reported being 'different people' in their second headship. As reported in Reeves and Dempster (1998), who you are, who you become, and how you change are all deeply affected by the context in which you work and the expectations that people hold of you.

> *Contextual factors meant that transfer of learning from one situation to another was not necessarily straightforward or helpful. They felt very strongly that the way in which a school leader operated had to be understood in this light. Context was highly significant and the same person, they argued, placed in different contexts acts differently because of different opportunities and constraints. (p. 155)*

Although the second-timers are, in a sense, still growing into and learning on the job, the second time around they are doing so with more confidence and clarity.

> *When you arrive at your second school you have to be careful not to assume things you put in place in your last school are in place here – it's a new school. The context has changed. In my first headship I had to create the agenda, but now you have to be ready to respond more sharply. The pressure is on as you walk through the door. Even though I knew a lot more when I started this job, I never stop learning. (Female secondary head, England)*

The second-timers were all convinced that what works in one school will not necessarily work in another.

> *It's different in this school from my last one. In my last headship I was more directive. That style was not appropriate here. (Male primary head, England)*

Leadership styles

The issue of leadership style was a predominant theme in the interviews with the 27 heads. They were asked how they would describe their own leadership style and how they thought others would describe them. Their responses can be categorised under three headings:

- Collaborative and collegiate
- Flexible and mixed
- Strong and up-front.

Collaborative and collegiate

While collaborative leadership was a common theme, there were different emphases, to some extent dependent on the size of the school, sector and culture. A headteacher of a New Zealand school referred to 'whanau', a Maori term for the extended family, very important in the Maori culture, to underline the importance of consensus in decision-making: 'We don't make decisions until everyone is in agreement', adding 'our collective vision is far greater than individual personalities'.

A nursery head expressed the view that in a small school there was no option.

In a little school it has to be co-operative and based on consensus. (Female nursery head, England)

Other heads spoke about participative management and shared leadership. Participative management was described in these terms by one primary head:

I feel very strongly about the importance of participative management and creating a culture that involves all staff and children which empowers them to grow personally. Everyone is a manager. I'm obsessively committed to trying to create positive attitudes. I think it is very important as a head to create a space for other people to talk about what's going on. (Male primary head, England)

A secondary head used the term 'multiple leadership' to describe his attempts to let different people in the school take the lead. Another secondary head, while advocating shared leadership, adds the following caveat:

I'm willing to listen but I am no wimp. (Female secondary head, USA)

Some heads recognised that a collaborative or democratic style was desirable but were not convinced that all their colleagues wanted to participate in decision-making.

I hope it's [leadership style] not autocratic though it's not totally democratic either. I am aspiring towards a corporate style of management. I give people the opportunity to give suggestions and share ideas. Some do it willingly and openly though some are just not ready to be equal parts of the team. I want us all to work together effectively to manage the change which is constantly coming our way. (Female primary head, England)

Others spoke of the difficulty of going against the grain of people's expectations. For teachers who had been used to a more authoritarian style of leadership, dependency could be more comfortable and more difficult to break out of. Again this was particularly pertinent for the head from South Africa.

I would like to think that I have a democratic approach to leadership, though this approach is not easy. It's difficult for teachers who have been used to an old-style authoritarianism. It's easy to criticise but a bit more difficult when you have to live with the decisions you make. The threat of accountability is very real when you cannot just blame others. Also democratic decision-making takes a lot of time. It particularly takes time to try and reach a consensus rather than just go for a majority decision.

Teachers have a very heavy workload and so more and more meetings after school are not always popular and the ethos of meetings has not previously been cultivated. Some staff are not familiar with meeting procedures and sometimes they suggest I make the decisions myself. In the old days when one person made the decisions you knew where to go to lobby if you did not agree with it. But once decisions are made by the whole staff they cannot be revoked by one person. Far more is expected of teachers now and some of them don't like that. (Male primary head, South Africa)

Flexible and mixed

Some of the heads suggested that they had a flexible approach to leadership and adopted a range of styles depending on the context. They believed that 'situational leadership' was the appropriate mode of leadership for heads – that is, adopting the style which is most fitting and most pragmatic for the job in hand:

My perspective relates to the job I've had to do. In a different kind of school the answer might be different. There are different styles of running schools and you have to be true to yourself, which is not always easy when some styles are in fashion. (Female secondary head, England)

'Situational leadership' is a term that has been used to describe the variation in styles of leadership to meet different demands and different contexts. Five of the women headteachers interviewed spoke about having a mix of styles and were aware that they did use different styles for different purposes. They could be consultative, autocratic, or *laissez-faire,* depending on the situation. Moving in and out of roles according to demand is described by one head in the following terms:

There are times when I need to be compassionate, gentle and thoughtful and other times when I need to be strategic, innovative and astute. I move in and out of roles according to what is demanded. (Female secondary head, Australia)

Different situations and different times need different approaches, said one secondary head. The challenge was 'knowing when to push and when to back off, when to give a strong lead and when to support'. A nursery head spoke about the need to be clear about what is and is not negotiable:

I have a framework of negotiables and non-negotiables so, for example, having respect for the children and their parents and believing that all our children are capable of wonderful things is not negotiable. The way we achieve this is. (Female nursery head, England)

Strong and up-front

A few of the heads did not believe that you could operate without a very up-front leadership style. As one headteacher put it, taking the money and doing the job you are required to do necessarily implied 'strong leadership'. Another outwardly rejected the notion of decision-making by consensus, adding:

I do not believe in decision-making by consensus but I do believe in listening and I can be influenced. I don't think you can have collective responsibility in a school. It's a bit like a ship's captain in a storm – you can't go into discussions in this situation: you need a strong helmsman. (Male primary head, England)

There is, in this account, a clear recognition of the 'I' who listens, makes the decisions and takes responsibility. The head whose deputy described her as a 'devious autocrat' is unashamed about making clear who is the boss and where responsibility for final decision-making lies:

I lead from the front but my deputy says I am a devious autocrat. When people apply to work in the school I am very clear about my style of leadership. I am the kind of person that, when the director of education says 'jump', I say 'how high?' I respect authority and have the same expectations of everyone else. Staff know exactly what I expect and why I expect what I expect. I do not ask them to do anything I would not do myself. I like to make sure that the staff are with me so I gather their opinions before I make a final decision. Some of our most successful initiatives have come from discussions at staff meetings. At first as a head you are unsure about your strengths – now I know what they are and I have learned to handle them better. (Female primary head, England)

Leading from the front meant being clear about the model of leadership you were offering, setting high expectations of yourself in order for others to follow. Some recognised this as a potential weakness:

I probably work too hard and I know I have appointed other people who work too hard – we know that's a danger. I have very high expectations of myself and other people. (Female primary head, England)

I have high expectations of myself and the staff. People probably think of me as a workaholic. (Male secondary head, England)

Common to all of these accounts is the recognition that the demands of leadership require flexibility of response. The responses required range from a recognition of push and pull, and an acknowledgement of the need to be clear about what is and is not up for negotiation. They also thought it was important for their colleagues to know where the leader stands and what the leader stands for.

Learning from and becoming models

Several of the heads spoke about the importance of modelling – how their behaviour gave important signals and clues to the adults and children they worked with.

The similarity in the following three quotes from men and women heads in different contexts illustrates a very similar way of thinking about the importance and functioning of modelling.

I think it's important to lead by example. The way you speak to people is very important. I try to treat everyone with respect, teaching and support staff, children and parents, and hope that they then do the same. (Female primary head, England)

I think 'modelling' in relationship to the children and the curriculum is vitally important. I try to work closely with teachers to show what is possible and what our children are capable of. (Male primary head, England)

He or she [the head] is also an important role model. For example how I relate to students is how I expect staff to relate to students. (Male special school head, England)

Modelling assumed particular significance for one of the black primary headteachers who saw herself as a role model for her pupils to aspire to. Her comment that her own role model had been her mother illustrates why modelling assumes such significance and how it is passed on from generation to generation.

My mother . . . was the first black headteacher in Wales. In spite of being told by her own teachers that she could never be a teacher because of her colour, she has been very successful. She has always felt strongly about the importance of education. (Female primary head, England)

As Peter and Jo Mortimore point out, the experience of being managed by others and observing those heads at work informs the way teachers attempt to behave when they assume that role. The irony is that it is often the negative role model that has the most potent influence.

Some poor role models taught me how not to do things. More positive models are Charles Handy who taught me at the business school has a great ability to write enlightening common sense. I take bits from all sorts of places from the Leadership Secrets of Attila the Hun and Peter Drucker to educational thinkers and academics including Peter Mortimore and David Reynolds. Also I believe that aspects of the way you seek to work are profoundly part of who you are and what you are, which is why leadership style is so different with different people and can be equally successful. (Female secondary head, England)

Stages in leadership

When you are a new head you can never imagine being an experienced one. (Female secondary head, England)

One of the primary heads interviewed had previously written about the stages of leadership, describing three stages which he called the autocratic, democratic and withdrawal stages. As a new head autocracy comes naturally and it is understandable and even perhaps necessary to assert the centrality of the head's position.

It has distinct virtues. It brings the staff together so that as a group, it identifies the position of the leader clearly, it creates security; psychologically, it is not far removed from the approach a new headteacher might take to a new class – the early days required a firm statement of the teacher's expectations. (Winkley, 1989, p. 17)

This does not, of course, give the head permission to 'plough furrows through the feelings of staff' and over time the head has to resist 'a dangerous totalitarian temptation to remain the boss' and, argues Winkley, it is dangerous for the school to remain fixated round this centrifugal point. So the leader has to work towards careful understanding of the meaning and context of the school if she wishes the school and staff to grow.

The third stage strengthens the autonomy of the group and the leader is able to withdraw, changing her role to allow staff to take the initiative, providing opportunities for leadership to be exercised by other members of staff. The role of the head becomes more of an advisory, evaluative one in which she can take part as an equal member of the group. Teamwork is a characteristic of this third mature phase.

Teamwork

The importance of working with teams was mentioned by several of the interviewees. The collective ownership of ideas is contained in the following account from a secondary head:

I hate the phrase 'my school' – I really do believe in teams. I can honestly say that I often do not know which ideas have come from me and which from the rest of the senior management team. (Male secondary head, England)

Others spoke about the importance to them personally of being part of a team, recognising their own weaknesses and relying on the team to add their strengths and synergy. Synergy and shared responsibility are illustrated in the following example from an American headteacher who described the creation of independent teams:

There is no way I can do all the things that need to be done without the help of staff. Everyone on my staff belongs to a design team (working party) which is independent of me. We have design teams for curriculum development, curriculum adoption, student success, teachers' well-being, community liaison, correspondence [communications], pupil support, resources and PTA. This leads to more synergy and shared responsibility. (Male primary head, USA)

Doing it 'with' rather than 'through' staff was how one secondary head described it, while another saw himself as 'the new Captain Kirk':

I try to work in teams. I see myself in the new rather than the old Star Trek style. The original Captain Kirk stayed on the bridge making decisions; the new one calls meetings. (Male secondary head, Wales)

Three of the explicit purposes of teamwork were to utilise the different talents available, get things done more effectively; and enhance professional development:

> *I like being part of a team and I'm a good starter, full of enthusiasm, but not so good at finishing, which is where the team is so important. (Female primary head, England)*

> *I believe in empowering other staff to take opportunities – for their own personal development but most importantly because this is the way to get things done effectively. You can't have an ego trip and believe that heads are the sole font of wisdom or the only ones that can do anything well. An effective school has a team approach. (Female secondary head, Scotland)*

> *It is important to be able to recognise and build leadership in others. For me it's building a community of learners and utilising the strengths of those around me. (Male primary head, USA)*

It was, in the view of some heads, a source of job satisfaction to see the growth, moving on and promotion of their colleagues. Three of the women heads spoke about the importance of, and enjoyment in, seeing others develop and creating the opportunities for them to do so:

> *I do genuinely enjoy seeing other people develop. (Female primary head, England)*

> *I believe in creating an environment where there are opportunities for other people to grow. It is very rewarding when people you work with get promotion and move on. (Female secondary head, England)*

> *I always encourage staff to develop themselves, professionally and personally. At the moment, two of us, out of a staff of nine, are doing masters courses. (Female primary head, England)*

The significance of the school itself as the prime site for learning is also a common theme. One primary head who described himself as 'a facilitator of learning' sees this as being achieved through a clear message to staff that they are valued and that where mutual trust and a learning climate exist, effectiveness can follow:

> *School must be a place where they [staff] are seriously valued. I don't expect to create personal friendships among the staff but do want to create relationships that allow us to trust and respect each other so that we can take the risks necessary to be more effective. We are all learners and my role is to facilitate the learning. (Male primary head, Canada)*

What is the most important aspect of the job?

There was a remarkable level of agreement among heads about the most important aspects of their jobs, regardless of their sex, country, or phase of school. There were three predominant themes:

- managing and motivating others
- creating an environment, or ethos, for people to grow and function more effectively
- establishing a direction and creating a vision.

'Leading', 'motivating', 'inspiring, and 'encouraging' were words used in describing the relationship with staff. However collegial those relationships, heads clearly saw a distinctive leadership role.

To make sure it is possible for teachers to do their job and that they do it. (Male primary head, Scotland)

Another primary headteacher recognised the delicate balance between leadership directed at children and leadership which is motivational for staff.

To lead and motive others [is the most important aspect of my job]. After I had been here for a short time one of the teachers told me that I cared about children more than the staff. It made me rethink what I was doing and I realised that an important part of my job is to manage people. Adults need your care as well. (Female primary head, Scotland)

A secondary head was convinced that his energies had to be devoted to staff:

No question. Working with staff. In the end the quality of education to kids is delivered in the classroom. The head has to make life more bearable for staff by making the working conditions better, creating resources, and supporting policies that set perimeters. It all depends upon what people are doing in the classroom. (Male secondary head, England)

Further light is thrown on this delicate balance by a secondary headteacher who emphasised that 'getting the best out of people' means not only support but confronting and raising expectations.

Getting the best out of people you work with: staff, children and parents. Some children come here from extraordinary circumstances. They need to feel secure and supported but not patronised. We expect the same standards from them as anyone else and the idea of low expectations because of disadvantage is anathema. (Male secondary head, England)

Getting the best out of people was seen by a number of heads as a process which comes through an ethos of opportunity, creating resources, 'conditions', 'environment', 'context' which enable people to work effectively and well.

To provide the context and opportunities for staff to make an effective contribution to the running of the school and to curriculum development. (Female secondary head, Scotland)

A good head creates the environment to allow other people to do their job to the best of their ability. (Male special school head, England)

> *Creating a school culture where the weakest member at any given time is being supported in their growth in the recognition that all of us including the principal, are the weakest member at some point in time. (Male primary head, Canada)*

Three male primary heads spoke about the importance of establishing and maintaining a vision.

> *Clarity of vision, knowing what a school could be like and being able in whatever way to communicate that. (Male primary head, England)*

> *To establish the direction and vision, ensure that there is a shared vision and a clarity of purpose which is to serve this community and help the children and their parents in every way we can. (Male primary head, Scotland)*

> *Leadership and vision. I've been in schools where everyone is doing their own thing and in schools where everyone is moving in the same direction. Both are hard. But by far, doing your own thing in isolation is much harder. (Male primary head, USA)*

What is the most enjoyable aspect of the job?

What is important and what is enjoyable may often coincide. Most of the heads spoke about loving the job, the satisfaction, the challenge and excitement which one head described as a 'privilege'. It was, according to a primary head, 'the best job in the world'. Asked what they enjoyed most about their job it was the 'people things' that came immediately to the fore – 'working with people', 'interaction', 'engagement' and 'sharing'. Regardless of the age group they were responsible for, most of the heads spoke about the pupils as the main source of their enjoyment:

> *I enjoy the interaction with kids and the variety. Every day is different . . . It's a good feeling helping kids and knowing that school is the only safe haven for some of them. (Male secondary head, Canada)*

Rather than seeing children as a drain on energy, they could be the *source* of energy, as one American head describes it.

> *I love being around young children and find that some of their energy transfers to me. When I'm stressed I head straight for the kindergarten. (Male primary head, Canada)*

Although the exhilaration of being with children was a predominant theme among primary heads, secondary heads also found it a source of personal and professional satisfaction to see children grow, through the teenage years and into adulthood.

> *Seeing children achieve and develop into confident young adults who feel at ease with themselves and the community they live in. (Male secondary head, England)*

> *I love teenagers; their excitement of life. They are fresh and honest with their feedback. They are at a stage in their lives when they are learning about themselves. (Female secondary head, Australia)*

> *Working with young people. There is a constant source of reward watching them develop and sharing their pleasure in the things they've achieved. Only in secondary schools do you get real engagement with young adults. They make extraordinary progress between the ages of eleven to eighteen. (Female secondary head, England)*

Meeting ex-pupils was also an important source of satisfaction for two of the primary heads. Being remembered, getting 'a pat on the back' was a tangible token that, however little feedback there may be during the school years, the long-term investment in young people's learning is eventually recognised and pays off:

> *In the summer I went to the retirement function of the head of my previous school. I met some of my ex-pupils who are now adults, had been to university and done really well. They remembered me as a good teacher. (Female primary head, England)*

> *My greatest enjoyment is when pupils from high schools come back and pat us on our backs. When they come back and ask us for advice it shows they still have confidence in us as teachers, even though they left us four or five years ago. (Male primary head, South Africa)*

The challenge, the opportunities, the variety, and the constantly evolving nature of the job prevented boredom and apathy. 'No two days are the same', 'no one day is the same as the next' were persistent themes, and although the job is demanding and stressful, as a headteacher you could 'make things happen'.

> *[I enjoy] Most of it! It's never boring, you deal with a huge variety of issues – a distressed child one moment and writing a policy the next. The job is fantastically varied – very demanding and very interesting. It's a privilege to see children developing with you. When you're a head you can make things happen for staff or for children. It's great! (Female secondary head, England)*

What is the most difficult and least enjoyable?

The most difficult aspects of the job turned out to be the least enjoyable too. There was considerable agreement about what this was:

- criticising staff
- dealing with redundancy
- selection and retention
- low status of teachers
- misinformation about state education
- administration
- pace of change
- lack of time.

Almost all the heads, regardless of their sex or phase, found criticising staff the most difficult thing they had to undertake as part of their job:

> *having to confront staff when things are not going according to plan. I want to be encouraging, praising and accentuating the positive, but sometimes there comes a time when you have to point out that someone's practice is not in line with our policies. It's difficult to balance my high expectations that everything will be perfect at all times, with the reality of school life which is tiring and challenging. (Female nursery head, England)*

> *It makes me sad when I have to criticise adults about something. I know I have to do it sometimes but I do not like hurting people and inside I am thinking this is really hard. (Female primary head, England)*

> *It's very rare but occasionally I've had to talk to a teacher about something that I do not like happening in a classroom which is against the ethos and beliefs of the school. (Female primary head, England)*

> *Having to confront other people with things that aren't going right and trying to do it in a way that helps people accept it and be able to grow through it. (Female secondary head, England)*

> *Dealing with disciplinary issues involving staff or students – making judgements about people that are so significant and important. (Male secondary head, England)*

The next most difficult and least enjoyable thing they had to face was making staff redundant.

> *In my first term of headship I had to make four staff redundant. If I had known that was going to happen I would not have applied for the job. For a long time after, understandably, staff were mistrustful of management and I had to work hard to change that. (Female nursery head, England)*

A few cited staffing selection and retention issues as the most difficult thing they did.

> *Not being able to keep young, eager, good teachers because of staffing constraints. Selecting for posts when there is more than one good candidate. (Female secondary head, Scotland)*

> *I find the process of selecting staff difficult too. We do it scrupulously but I don't relish the process of selection because it means rejection and that sometimes includes good people because there are not enough vacancies. (Male secondary head, England)*

> *I find staff selection very hard, probably because I'm aware how important it is. (Male special school, England)*

The heads, particularly the men, were very unhappy about the status of teachers in society and the amount of misinformation about state schools that was current.

> *The status of teachers, which has been undermined and can only make the job more difficult. I think raising the status of teachers is even more important than an increase in salaries. (Male secondary head, England)*

We are suffering from chronic centralisation of the intellectual agenda. There's a sense in which we're under siege from people who don't teach and who treat teachers with subliminal contempt. I worry about the nature of power of men in these centralist positions – most of them are men and most people in teaching are women. Teachers have been disenfranchised from the debate. They are like the First World War troops in the trenches. I'm not complacent about schools; we've hardly tapped into what children can do, but this is not the way forward and not the way to encourage young people into the profession. (Male primary head, England)

The frustration of having the wrong story told about education. Having to spend huge amounts of time dispelling untruths and fighting against the consequences of the disparagement of the British system. I often wonder why the brightest and best young people would ever want to come into teaching given what they hear about it although it is in reality one of the most wonderful jobs. (Male secondary head, England)

This view was not restricted to the UK contingent. It was echoed by a Canadian head too.

The amount of criticism and misinformation that is around about education. Schools are blamed for every ill of society. Plus [I do not enjoy] the paperwork, lack of funding and political interference. (Male secondary head, Canada)

Most of the primary heads mentioned administration as one of their main dislikes.

I think I'm a teacher rather than a head so I find the administration difficult. I've discovered that if you leave it for a long time a lot of it becomes out of date. (Female nursery head, England)

Paperwork. Sometimes I come in and want to burn it all. (Female primary head, England)

The pace of change and the lack of time to do the job were mentioned frequently as pet hates.

Not having enough time to engage in the remarkable number of things teachers have to deal with. Some changes have been needed but the pace of change and the lack of resources to support change have not been helpful. (Male secondary head, England)

Lack of time to do things and so not being able to achieve all you want to. (Female secondary head, England)

A few heads did not enjoy having so little time for themselves and complained about finding it difficult to find time for thinking. Again, this was not just the English:

Staying on top of everything and taking time for myself. (Male secondary head, Canada)

And one experienced head (who has since left headship) was worried about how long you can sustain the role:

keeping going. The pure remorselessness of the job can be demanding and worrying. (Male primary head, England)

Managing the budget was an additional cause of concern for one secondary and two primary heads.

One of the heads interviewed after the first round of OFSTED inspections was clear that she had not enjoyed the experience of being inspected.

Although we got an excellent report, I did not enjoy the pressure that the OFSTED inspection put us under. I could not believe how much it affected me and the staff. Once it was over I thought it was wrong and felt abused by the process even though some good things came out of it. We stood still for a year. We did not develop, we just polished things that were already excellent. During that time we did not grow as a school. We are now growing again. (Female primary head, England)

Given another chance . . .

The heads were asked if they would have done anything differently, knowing what they know now. Almost all of them mentioned pacing themselves differently, not being so impatient, doing some things a little slower and others a little quicker.

Be more focused and more realistic. Not to expect changes to happen immediately. (Female primary head, England)

As a new head you try too hard – you can kill yourself or burn yourself out. I worked very hard and got very tired. (Female primary head, England)

Pace myself a bit better, the first few years were very draining and demanding. I would learn not to be frustrated that you cannot do everything at once. (Female secondary head, Scotland)

Be a bit less conscientious. When I came to the school it had to be changed; it was 'do or die' and extraordinarily hard work. A lot of fun though! I'm not sure I could do it differently. (Female secondary head, Scotland)

Loads of things. Particularly space things out better, be a bit less urgent and obsessional and not allow myself to get so over-tired. (Female primary secondary head, England)

And finally, one of the interviewees summed up what he thought were the essential attributes of a successful head.

I try and have a sensitive heart but the skin of a rhinoceros. (Male primary head, England)

4

The Dilemmas of Leadership

With the arrival of a new headteacher, schools can 'turn around' and move from disaster to triumph. Losses are turned into gains. Low achievement becomes high achievement. The new head knows what to do to put things right because there is an unwritten rulebook of good, and even 'best', practice.

Viewed from a distance this seems to describe what actually happens, and the gloss in the literature and the rhetoric of the politician endorses that neat and tidy state of the art. Headteachers who have had an impact on schools, however, tell a different story. The Effective Leadership study (MacBeath, 1998) which included 40 heads from four countries, explored the anxiety, the stress, the dilemmas, the human side of leadership. It failed to find a golden rulebook or recipe for effective leadership but did identify ways of increasing our understanding of, and response to, dilemmas.

A common response among headteachers, no matter their country of origin, was to assume a mask of efficiency and confidence. Their dilemmas were dealt with behind their office door, often a very lonely place. Angus Macdonald, a Scottish headteacher who was a participant in that study, described how you can fool most of the people most of the time. Whether as a conscious strategy or simply by virtue of status and position, staff, parents and pupils assume that a head knows what he or she is doing. He or she is seen as operating in a rational and strategic manner, weighing the evidence, considering alternatives, drawing on considered knowledge of the school and its community, behaving rationally and with forethought. The reality, says Angus Macdonald, is nothing like this. Drawing on his own experience as a headteacher, he proposes the matrix shown in Figure 4.1.

Leaders, he suggests (Macdonald, 1998), quite often make decisions and judgements in the condition of surprise. This is an ability admired and valued by others. But he writes:

Figure 4.1: Macdonald's matrix
(*Source*: Macdonald (1998))

> *In this condition, the leaders surprise themselves. It occurs where a new situation has arisen and the leader is surprised to find himself or herself reacting with a sense of sureness of touch, of knowing just what to do and then doing it. It is as though the leader was unaware of what he or she knew until the situation itself demanded the response and he found it already formed. It may be to do with unarticulated knowledge, or it may be to do with the ability to see through the detail of the situation to the fundamental issues, and then to apply the relevant principles to produce a resolution. Whatever, it is much prized by others because it conveys a sense of ability to 'think on one's feet', or of a very profound depth of experience. It inspires confidence and trust. For this reason, the wise leader will keep his or her sense of surprise well hidden and will look exactly as they would have, had they been aware of this all along. (p. 167)*

In terms of how it looks from the outside, this (quadrant 2 of Figure 4.1) is virtually indistinguishable from quadrant 1. Perhaps, suggests Macdonald, this is why it is so seldom acknowledged. It is in quadrant 3, anxiety, that, he claims, most decisions and judgements are made. Many situations do not allow a headteacher time to research all the things she should do and should know about, but shrewd leadership means minimising the uncertainty as far possible, consolidating, developing fall-back positions, 'staging' any commitment to the decision, to allow flexibility of response as more information emerges. None the less, Macdonald continues:

> *the degree of uncertainty creates anxiety and the more the leader is aware of what he or she does not know, the greater the anxiety will be. This condition also can lead to the paralysis of leadership, because it can of course affect the individual to a major degree; this is why leadership requires real courage. One of the most difficult tasks a leader has is to sustain both flexibility of response and the belief in the outcome that*

> *inspired the decision in the first place, during the gap between the commitment to the decision and the realisation of the outcome itself. Anything that goes wrong within this time gap, however unconnected it may seem to be, tends to be linked to the original decision, especially if it was contentious. The leader must uphold and defend the decision while bearing in mind the possibility that the connection might, in truth, be there. (p. 168)*

There is a close parallel with David Hargreaves's matrix (Figure 4.2). Hargreaves (1998) distinguishes 'recognised knowledge', 'recognised ignorance', 'unrecognised knowledge' and 'unrecognised ignorance'. The last of these is Macdonald's state of 'bliss' (quadrant 4 in Figure 4.1). But as Macdonald says, it is also the *terra incognita*, the rock on which leadership may perish.

> *If this were a Mediaeval Management Matrix, this quadrant would be clearly marked 'Terra Incognita' and 'Here be Monsters' for this is truly unknown territory and monsters do lurk here – the monstrously unlucky, the monstrously unlikely and the monstrously unfair – and they can take any form. Every leader carries this 'Terra Incognita' into every situation, however familiar, or new, it may appear; this condition is so all-pervading and permanent that we cease to recognise it and we operate in practice often as though it does not exist. Perhaps this is necessary or else leadership would really be paralysed; except that good leadership allows for it and takes action. (p. 168)*

In the blissful state *terra incognita* is devoid of dilemma. The dilemmas occur very explicitly in quadrant 2 – when we become aware of our own ignorance. But they also occur in quadrant 1 – becoming fully aware of what we know but then paralysed by that very knowledge. It has been said that to know all is to forgive all, and that is a far more problematic state psychologically than the bliss of quadrant 4.

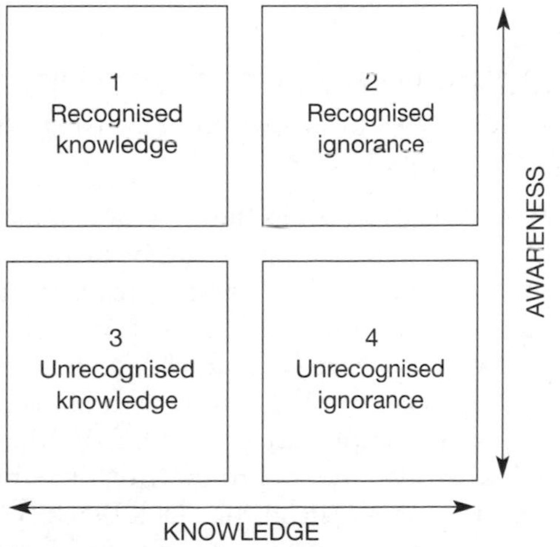

Figure 4.2: Hargreaves's matrix
(*Source*: Hargreaves (1998))

In the study that Angus Macdonald describes, headteachers did not find it easy to explore in depth with one another their most acute ethical dilemmas. Perhaps they did not know each other well enough to dig too deeply into those private struggles. Perhaps the issues raised were too painful and personal to revisit in depth. Interviews with the research team did, however, offer a more confidential and safe context, and exploration of diaries and spontaneous informal discussions revealed many of the anxieties that headteachers face. As researchers, we were sometimes admitted into that lonely place where dilemmas are resolved and decisions made, sometimes agonisingly.

At these moments of weighing the balance, often intuitively rather than with an array of considered alternatives, headteachers had recourse to their fundamental values in guiding their actions. Where there was a conscious counterbalancing of options, the dilemmas were framed in terms of competing principles:

- children's entitlement or good financial housekeeping?
- targeting children who might improve the school's position in the league tables or attending to those with the greatest learning difficulties?
- the good of the school as a whole or one's own personal kudos?

This wrestling with the complexities of ethical decision-making is an important, enduring and increasing feature of professional life. That is the conclusion of researchers who have explored beneath the surface of headteacher behaviour. A recent study by Clive Dimock (1996) in Australia concluded that situations were more likely to be perceived as dilemmas when four conflicting conditions were present:

- there was an expectation of, or perceived need for, a successful resolution;
- the leader would personally have to shoulder the responsibility for the outcome;
- there was a commensurate lack of control or influence over the outcome;
- there was a high degree of incompatibility between resolving the issue and attainment of other desired goals.

In other words, there was, inherent in the situation, a counterpoint of conflicting expectations, 'not only from the outside but from the inside too', as one headteacher put it. From the outside, parents, teachers, students and governing bodies looked to certain outcomes, to assured leadership, but also to a listening and receptive ear. There was a desire to be consulted and involved and at the same time a wish for authoritative and conviction-led decision-making. Conflicting sets of expectations came from the inside too, from 'the internalised others', from the inner board of directors who could at times push and pull in different directions. The author Jack Black (1994) describes the tensions from his own personal inner board which, he says, includes Richard Branson, Billy Connolly and Jesus Christ.

Clive Dimock classified dilemmas in two ways. There are those that revolve around tensions of personal role, status and position. Then there are those that are concerned with the purposes and functions of schooling, its structures and processes, its curriculum, the nature of teaching and learning, and the flow of resources. The second set of dilemmas has greatly increased as a consequence of educational restructuring, but they bring in their wake a sharpening of the first set of dilemmas too.

Examples of dilemmas to do with role and status include the following:

- To what extent am I personally accountable for the short-term attainment outcomes of my pupils? How do I reconcile this with my own priorities to help staff focus on lifelong learning?
- To what extent am I the director of a self-managing school and to what extent an agent of external bodies (the local authority, the Department, the Government)?
- Is my first duty to the internal community of the school, to the external community, or to parents?
- To what extent should I maintain and preserve the *status quo,* and to what extent should I be the initiator of change?
- Should I emphasise school evaluation for development and improvement purposes or for accountability?

Dilemmas to do with restructuring include:

- How do I maintain the traditional structures but introduce new ways of working?
- How do I preserve status and position while challenging hierarchy and rigid adherence to authority?
- How can staff morale be maintained in the face of limited opportunities to offer incentives and rewards?
- How do I empower parents and students without disempowering or threatening teachers?
- How do I find the balance between academic/cognitive and personal/social development?
- How do I encourage a more effective use of time and resources when both are in increasingly short supply?

Dimock's separation of these two sets of dilemmas is in some senses an arbitrary one since both rest on basic values, on such questions as 'what is the moral purpose of education?' and 'what scope and responsibility do I carry for realising that moral purpose?'

Those moral purposes are, perhaps, best understood in terms of stability and change, the tension between stable moral values and unstable social norms. The impulse which took someone into teaching, and ultimately into a position of leadership, may sit uncomfortably with how that role is being redefined in a changing national and international context. The roots of the dilemma have their origins in those first uncomplicated days and weeks in the learning classroom.

The origins of ethical dilemmas – the classroom teacher

When considerations of security, salary and career are set to one side, the common driving motivation to be a teacher is to bring about a change in the lives of children and young people. As in medicine, counselling, social and community work, there is one underpinning value position – to bring about changes that are in the client's own best interests. As Neil Dempster (1998) describes it, the surgeon alters the physical status of patients by operating on their bodies in order to improve their health; the psychologist aims to bring about improvements in a client's mental health by means of specialised conversations; and the teacher provides experiences that will help children to make the transition to more informed and effective adults. The headteacher orchestrates relationships and environment so as to allow teachers and pupils to learn and grow together.

It is when these deep moral purposes seem to be compromised by pragmatic and political considerations that dilemmas begin to surface. The young teacher with her first class may experience an initial exhilaration: 'This is what I came into teaching for.' Learning and teaching is all that exists in her world, and there is a pristine simplicity in the blossoming relationship of teacher and learners. With time, however, things change. Other considerations begin to loom larger. There are demands from outside – demands on monitoring attendance, formal assessment, tracking progress, marking and returning homework, chasing the miscreants, threatening and employing sanctions, having recourse to higher authorities to intervene, keeping up with the imperatives of a changing curriculum. There is a shifting perception of role from 'me in my classroom' to 'us in the school'. You are no longer a teacher in a classroom with your door closed, but a member of a corporate enterprise in which teaching is not your own and in which even you are not your own.

The internal honeymoon relationship within the classroom undergoes a change too, sometimes sooner rather than later. The term lengthens, the nights become longer, the weather worsens. There are shifts in relationships within the classroom. It becomes a more complex place. The lives of children begin to unfold in greater complexity. There is neither the time nor the permission to get to 'know' the 30 children let alone the 150 or 200 that a secondary teacher may see in the course of a week. Keeping distance is the first rule and one that, when breached, leads to a tortured place.

The moral dilemmas of the classroom have been portrayed vividly in first-hand accounts of teachers. The imperative of distance is vividly described by

Gary Cornog (1970) in the collection of essays entitled *Don't Smile Until Christmas*.

> *It seemed to me that I became more effective as I became less genuine as an individual. When I had periodic lapses into my actual personality I felt these were invariably detrimental in my attempt to teach. They hurt me because they made me vulnerable to attempts by the students to fraternise. Fraternisation made objectivity difficult for me and totally destroyed my credibility as an enforcer of discipline in the class. (p. 15)*

In his book *The Way it Spozed to be* James Herndon (1968) describes the massive inertia he faced in trying to move beyond the conservative expectations of his pupils. 'That's not the way it spozed to be, Mr Herndon', was their reflex response to any attempt to innovate, to challenge, to bend the expectations of a class of black children in a Harlem junior high school.

The tension between inspirational teaching and way it 'spozed' to be continues as a common strand as classroom teachers move on to become departmental heads, deputy heads and headteachers. While they may not always want to, they experience a strong need to move up the ladder and to move progressively away from the prime motive which brought them into the profession. While a few may be relieved to escape from the classroom, leaders tend to be chosen from those who made a success of classroom teaching. As heads, they want to keep their connections with teaching and learning, with children and young people. Most of the English and Scottish heads in our study wanted to spend time with children. They were interested in learning. This was particularly true of primary heads. Most didn't want to be managers or chief executives. They didn't want to spend their time on paperwork, policy and politics. Yet they found they had to give priority to external relationships, to manoeuvring and negotiation, to compromise and ingratiation.

In Chapter 2 we described the dilemma of the Chicago principals. These American heads had grown away from their roots. They were gradually losing touch with the motivations that had brought them into the profession. The balance of work has shifted, highlighting deep-seated tensions between maintenance and development, between managing and leading schools. As reported by studies of leadership in other countries, principalship find the job a lonely one.

Thomas Sergiovanni (1992) writes:

> *The most dramatic change in moving from your staff position into a leadership role is the loss of peers . . . promotion also diminishes support. You will not always have to respond entirely alone but you will usually have to respond first and orchestrate the response of others who will take their cue from you and most key leadership decisions, especially sensitive ones, are made in relative isolation. (p. 151)*

The dilemma of the headteacher is decision-taking in isolation and with a keen eye to the 'way it spozed to be'. So, like new teachers, new heads may try not to move too fast but experience the forces of inertia pushing them to conserve while innovating, stabilise while changing, bend while remaining unbending. The world-wide trend to devolve responsibility to the individual school and thence to the person of the head – where the buck stops – simply intensifies the dilemma.

Managing devolution

The American terminology of 'site management' puts the nature of the dilemma in stark terms. The 'site' is a large complex physical space demanding constant vigilance and maintenance. It is occupied by adults and children representing most of the age spectrum, a cross-cut of the socio-economic population, bringing with them day on day the full gamut of social problems into this compact arena. Security from the world outside, policing of the world inside, managing personnel, ensuring financial viability and long-term sustainability are the bottom-line preoccupations from which many headteachers and principals never manage to escape.

The devolution of authority to the school site is perhaps the most acute source of the ambivalence in leadership. It goes variously by the name of LMS – local management of schools, DSM – devolved school management, SBM – site-based management or SBL – site-based leadership. In the measure that it has brought increased latitude and powers to school senior management, it has commensurately increased accountability. And dilemma.

In the Effective Leadership study heads were asked to identify their dilemmas, to describe them, and then to join with others in finding ways of addressing them. This helped them to recognise that their dilemmas were not free-standing roadblocks but were closely interconnected. This information helped the heads deal with the dilemmas that had to be dealt with in the knowledge and understanding of their contextual interrelationship.

The following identifies the four main dilemmas.

Dilemma 1

In all countries school leaders faced the issue of what to do with underperforming or 'incompetent' staff. In England the difficulties have been exacerbated by the high political profile given to the issue in recent years under both Conservative and New Labour governments. It has become increasingly acceptable to use the language of 'incompetence' to refer to teachers, and taking a tough line on individual teachers is seen as equally justifiable as in any business context where poor performance is intolerable.

For some headteachers this eased rather than heightened the dilemma because it recognised and endorsed the validity of their problem. It gave them hope that someone or somebody might come along like a *deus ex machina* and painlessly extract the troublesome member. This was seen by some as a benefit of OFSTED and if OFSTED's interventions were viewed more positively by heads than by teachers, it was because of this mandate from an external authority against poor teaching.

However, OFSTED's interventions did not necessarily address the ethical dilemma for heads who were conscious of their own complicity or collusion. One problem for heads is that they have also been teachers and can identify with the dilemmas that teachers face at classroom level. They have been there themselves.

Empathy is an important attribute of good leaders but its strong moral content only exacerbates the dilemma, and leaders have to remind themselves from time to time of the first rule of teaching – measured distance. One head expressed the view that it was a no-win situation because to identify, to empathise, meant losing the critical distance, but to distance oneself too much risked compromising the human supportive quality of the relationship. Michael Fullan (1997b, p. 7) says about teachers, 'the more that they become emotionally detached the poorer the decisions they make'. This may also hold true for headteachers.

Dilemma 2

The issue of how to deal with 'incompetent' teachers is related to the second dilemma, expressed as frequently in the Effective Leadership study as among a study of Chicago principals. It has to do with what is described in the USA as 'outcome-based education'. In many countries during the late 1980s and early 1990s governments shifted the educational policy focus from concern for inputs to concern for outcomes. Measures of student achievement became critical yardsticks of how parents and members of the public were enjoined to make judgements about a school's performance. One English headteacher in the study expressed it in this way:

> *We know that we lose quite a number of good local students to other schools in the city because their parents see our results in the League Table – results which, because of our student base, place us in the bottom third of the list. The Council wants to set aside some money from this year's budget to offer ten students from our local primary schools a substantial bursary to attend this school. This money would be taken from the little we have at our discretion and I am troubled by the 'gung-ho' manner in which Council members are discussing a decision which they say will lift our standards. (English headteacher)*

The 'student base' which this head refers to is the social and educational capital of the students refined through aggregated measures of ability of the whole student body. A 'poorly performing school' is one in which those aggregated measures compare unfavourably with other schools. In their book *Good School, Bad School* John Gray and Brian Wilcox (1995) argue that 'raw' exam or test results 'run the distinct risk of rewarding schools for the "quality" of the intakes they can attract rather than what they actually do for pupils'. Quality is treated as synonymous with measured attainment and human beings are treated as some kind of inferior commodity. When figures are then presented to parents as a yardstick by which they can choose schools, it sets in train a downward spiral, a self-fulfilling prophecy, in which poorly performing schools become further impoverished. The nature of the self-fulfilling prophecy has been well documented by school effectiveness researchers for more than a decade. It has been described as the 'compositional effect', which shows that the more a school is drained of its motivated and high-achieving pupils, the greater the downward drag on those who remain. This point is illustrated in MacBeath (1999):

> *the point at which individual achievement falls or rises depending on who your peers are and how many of them are high or low achievers. As Douglas Willms showed in the Scottish context, when high achieving pupils leave, some of the school's positive energy source is drained off. Further, when high achieving pupils leave to go to a 'better' school, they may also take with them their more assertive parents and further drain the school of a potential energy or irritant source. (p. 13)*

Whether or not school leaders are conversant with the research or the technical concepts, they recognise intuitively and through experience the reality of the importance of intake and the danger of the self-fulfilling prophecy. It is the very awareness of the multi-dimensional nature of the issue that lies at the heart of the dilemma.

Dilemma 3

While much has been made of the isolation of the headteacher, decision-making is not always his or her province. While accountability for outcomes may rest with them, the control over decisions is not necessarily theirs. English headteachers have governing bodies, some of whom are all too willing to defer to the head's judgement but sometimes are also ready to challenge judgements in a way that is not only time-consuming but also contentious. The following dilemma, from a report by the National Association of Head Teachers (NAHT), England and Wales (Rafferty, 1995), illustrates this issue:

> *The growth in the number of disputes with governing bodies is causing alarm, with the union reporting an increase in the number of heads under suspension . . . heads were being suspended because they did not see eye-to-eye with their governing bodies and because inspections were creating a 'football-manager syndrome', where the head has to carry the can for poor reports and low league-table placings. (p. 1)*

In one school in the Effective Leadership study, a governing body had made a decision in the head's absence. The head, seeing this as running counter to his values and his goals for the school, presented a paper to the governing body. It expresses the frustration that Csikszentmihalyi (1990, p. 7) says is 'deeply woven into the fabric of life'. This was the head's paper:

Head's Expectations of the Governing Body

(1) To be always aware that they are partners, with staff, parents and the community, through the local authority, in providing the best education possible for the children who attend the school they govern.

(2) To recognise that although they have been given the ultimate responsibility and authority for the management of the school, the fundamental responsibility in practice rests with the headteacher and the staff.

(3) To recognise that their value to the partnership is directly proportional to:–

a) their knowledge and understanding of the process of education
b) their awareness of current issues that relate to the education system
c) their knowledge and experience of how the school is managed and how the children are educated
d) their relationships with all the other partners
e) their knowledge and understanding of the children's needs.

(4) To recognise that a) to e) demand a commitment of time and energy that has to be prioritised so that they are able to offer what most benefits the education of children.

The report from the NAHT has its own evidence of governors 'stepping over the mark', at least as seen from a headteacher perspective:

we do not find it acceptable for a head to return to the office to find governors who have gone through files and then make comments about the headteacher's efficiency . . . governors should leave the day-to-day running of schools to the head, but those who are happy to take the lead from the head when things are going well should not then dissociate themselves when things go wrong. Delegates complained that some governors liked the power, but walked away from responsibility. (Rafferty, 1995, p. 2).

From the governors' side, however, comes the counter-argument:

Governors are not just heads' supporters clubs. In many cases they do not do all their tasks and the head moves into the vacuum. But where they do take on their full role, they find the head does not like it. (National Association of Governors)

From the head's viewpoint, the dilemma is created by a failure to grasp the differences between strategic and operational issues, those things that are the province of governors and those things that belong in the province of the head. Drawing a clear line in the sand between these two proves, however, not to be a simple matter. Neat distinctions may lie in the domain of logic but, like all dilemmas, the solution also lies in the emotional and moral arena.

Dilemma 4

'Problem students' was one of the roadblocks identified by Chicago principals. Others might have expressed the same issue somewhat differently. They might have talked about 'students with problems' or 'problems created socially' or even by the school itself. All of these have a perennial quality but they have taken a more acute form in the 1990s. The pervasiveness and perniciousness of the 'drug culture' is a new phenomenon and the dilemmas created by it have also to be seen in the context of the three issues discussed above.

Drug abuse among young people is viewed with horror by most parents, and schools tread a wary line, anticipating the exposé by a sensationalist press. The following dilemma, articulated by an English headteacher in the study, illustrates the tension between the marketplace of public relations and the need to address an important educational issue:

> *I dare not admit publicly that we've got a drugs problem in the school in case it damages our reputation. This would mean that we would lose pupils and therefore funding. Yet, if I don't admit it we can't undertake a concerted effort with the parents and support services to tackle it properly. Neither do I want to permanently exclude the offending students as other schools have done even though I know that would improve our reputation. (English headteacher)*

Seeking solutions

How, then, are dilemmas resolved? They tend to be resolved pragmatically, 'on the hoof', often with retrospective *Angst* – Was it the right decision? What could have been done differently? Critical incident analysis is one useful tool in helping to take a more objective and systematic view so that it is possible to learn from mistakes as well as successes. Understanding critical incident analysis helps people to stand back from the event and unpack it in detailed sequence. This can identify where the key points of decision-making lie, and raise issues about influences on decision-making. With the wisdom of hindsight it is possible to ask – 'What could have been done differently?', 'Who was best placed to do that?', 'What would I/we do differently next time?'

Another useful strategy is 'reframing'. Like critical incident analysis, this can be used in hindsight to revisit a situation and see it in a different light. Better still, it can be used prospectively at the point of decision-making. The metaphor of the 'frame' is a useful one. The theory is that in any situation we enter we put a frame around it. Like a photograph it is 'snapped' from a chosen angle, mentally cropped beforehand (and perhaps physically cropped afterwards) to tell a story, convey an image, contained and bounded on four sides. This focuses our attention on key features. The frame defines what we see and, both helpfully and unhelpfully, limits what we see. Without the frame it is difficult to interpret events, but with the frame in place it can be understood more easily in terms of past events or with reference to other similar scenes from our recorded experience. The kind of frame we choose for any given situation will, however, vary according to all kinds of historical and psychological factors. It may or may not be the appropriate frame for that particular situation, and when we don't frame it appropriately we may be led towards the wrong conclusions.

Bolman and Deal (1991) have written extensively on the subject of reframing, applying the principle to organisations, roles and goals, motives and motivation. They identify four kinds of frame:

- the structural frame
- the human resource frame
- the political frame
- the symbolic frame.

The first kind, the structural frame, views the organisation in terms of goals and roles. It is concerned with strategic management issues, the vertical command structure and the lateral informal structures. A headteacher walking through the entrance hall and witnessing a scene of disorder might interpret what she sees in terms of 'Who is in charge here?' 'What rules are being broken?'

The human resource frame sees things more in terms of needs and motives. It perceives an environment in which people's behaviour is shaped by their expectations, satisfactions and priorities. Coming upon disorder from this point of view, the headteacher may immediately wonder what sets of environmental conditions or interactions have provoked this and can explain it. How might the environment be changed to redress the situation?

The political frame focuses on authority, resources, struggles for influence and power, bargaining, trade-off and compromise. If the disorderly conduct is viewed from this political frame, the headteacher may instinctively think in terms of win–lose or win–win, preserving her own authority, while also saving face for others.

The fourth and final frame, the symbolic frame, looks for meaning and symbols. It sees in metaphors, ritual and ceremony. It tries to understand situations with terms of deeper values such as trust, hope, commitment and faith. The head with this mind-set may feel deeply disappointed that her trust appears to have been betrayed and may feel that disorder is simply pointing towards some deeper unfulfilled human need to be addressed rather than dealing only with its surface manifestations.

Framing is both an instinctive and a learned response. The instinctive response to a meeting with a gorilla is to frame it as a flight, or fight, situation. The Jane Goodalls of the world, who have lived with gorillas, have acquired a quite different framing response. Their way of seeing has been learned and then internalised as a habit of insight. So reframing in school leadership can also become habitual, a way of responding instinctively and intuitively in that moment when a decision has to be made. The school leader who has acquired the ability to view things through many frames is in possession of the tool of 'multi-framing'. Her advantage is in seeing the situation simultaneously through a number of different lenses.

Reframing offers new insights. That is an intrinsically valuable asset for school leaders. But it need not stop there because reframing almost always requires that action follows. In common with other leadership gurus, Steven Covey (1989) advocates the logical extension of this as going for the 'win–win'. Indeed, Covey describes the 'win–win' as 'a frame of mind'. It is one that

> *constantly seeks mutual benefit in all human interactions. Win–win means that agreements or solutions are mutually beneficial, mutually satisfying. With a win–win solution, all parties feel good about the decision and feel committed to the action plan. A person with a win–win attitude sees life as a co-operative not a competitive arena. (p. 207)*

We might test the tools of reframing and the 'win–win' by applying them to the dilemmas above. How might we see the incompetence issue (dilemma 1) differently? Figure 4.3 illustrates a tool that has been used in a management context to categorise staff. It has an immediate appeal to management because it is easy to begin to slot people into their niche. We might even say it 'frames' them beautifully. The act of doing so, however, is likely to freeze them more permanently into that posture. Reframing would take them out of the frame and offer them four possible choices of frame, dependent on time of day, week, year, or dependent on mood, context, events, relationships. Aren't we all deadbeats at some time or other? Aren't we all go-getters in some aspects of our personal and professional lives? Haven't we all got subversive and political tendencies when it seems appropriate?

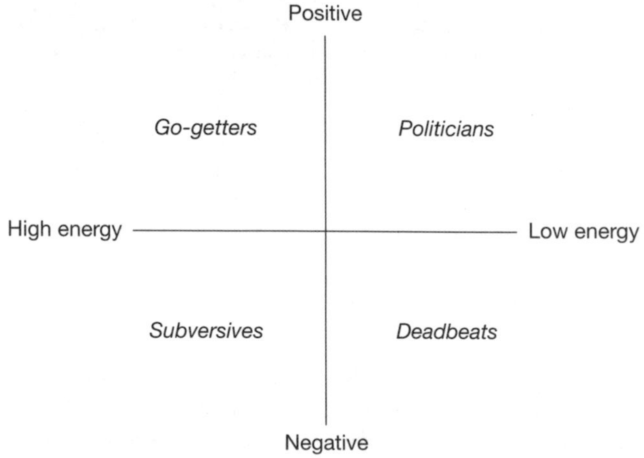

Figure 4.3: The framing grid

Rather than looking at the qualities of the individual as if they were inherent, the reframing (Figure 4.4) looks at the situation which constrains people to act in certain ways. It moves from Bolman and Deal's structural frame to the human resource frame. Reframing the issue of incompetence involves a shift of focus away from the portrait to the landscape, removing the individual as the central figure and focusing instead on the wider scene.

Ted Wragg (1998) warns against too easy an acceptance of the kind of labelling that comes easily to the lips of politicians and journalists. In an attempt to redress the lack of research evidence on the subject, he is concluding a two-year study, the Teaching Competence project, which is amassing evidence from 1800 interviews and 650 case studies. He finds evidence that so-called 'incompetent teachers' may be viewed as 'competent' in another school context. He warns of the danger of ascribing the perceived competence or incompetence to the inherent qualities of the individual rather than to the context in which they find themselves, or to the interaction between the individual and their behaviour setting.

This is not to deny that there are, by virtually all measures, teachers who should not be in schools. There are those who have given up or become disillusioned, their ingrained cynicism and antipathy to their own learning and professional development having managed to survive the decades. There are teachers who, by their own admission, cannot exercise their own will over thirty young people, yet cling on through suffering for want of other alterna-

1. Individually write the name of a place, a time of day/week/year, an activity or event which makes you feel positive/high energy, negative/low energy and so on.
2. Come together as a group to discuss what you have written. Identify three things that might be done to shift negatives to positives.

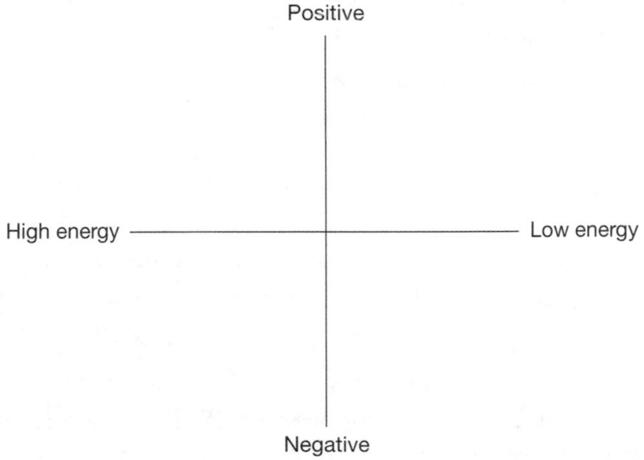

Figure 4.4: A staff exercise in reframing

tives. This does not invalidate the attempt to seek a 'win–win'. Some of these teachers might be excellent in different roles or within different kinds of structures and in different kinds of relationship, perhaps in individual tutoring, mentoring or study support. A key point in relation to seeking the win–win is, in Covey's terms, some investment in the emotional bank account. When that is not present it is probably a futile waste of energy to try for the win–win, and the win–lose may be in the interests of all but the immediate loser.

For example, the drug issue (dilemma 4) could be reframed in this way:

Old frame

- What is the problem? – Drugs
- Who are the problem? – Students who use drugs, students who sell drugs, the media, parents
- What is my problem? – The reputation of the school, what people will think
- What are my feelings about it? – Apprehensive, angry at market forces
- How am I behaving? – Reactive, dishonest
- What is my strategy? – Deny? Conceal? Gloss?

New frame

Reframing and looking for the win–win (Figure 4.5) might lead the head to turn the situation round by being proactive, enlisting the help of students and parents, contacting the media and having a story to tell:

The school that turned its back on drugs

Britain's first drug-free school?

Young people declare war on drugs

Parents and pupils unite against drugs

Raising the standard – Healthy Living Centres

- Who are the allies? – Students who don't use drugs, students who do use drugs, parents of students who don't use drugs, parents of students who do use drugs, the LEA, the health authority, the government, business, funding charities
- What is the opportunity? – To use this as a stimulus for everyone to learn
- What are my feelings about it? – Apprehensive, excited at the possibilities
- How am I behaving? – Proactively, honestly, politically
- Who are the potential winners? – Everyone
- What is my strategy? – Engaging people with the issues, forming alliances to confront the issues honestly and openly.

1 Identify the dilemma
2 Reframe
3 Consider:
- What would win–lose look like?
- What would a lose–win look like?
- What would a lose–lose look like?
- What would a win–win look like?
- How to get there

Figure 4.5: Going for the win–win

In conclusion

There are no simple one-fits-all solutions to the dilemmas which heads experience. The shifting sands on which their schools are founded, the capricious social norms and the changing expectations around them require ways of seeing and thinking rather than ready recipes. Reframing and thinking win–win are examples of how dilemmas may begin to point to their own solutions and can at least help heads to glimpse a way through.

Appendix 4.1
Frames of reference for dealing with an ineffective teacher

	Neither ethical nor practical	*Practical but unethical*	*Unethical but practical*	*Both ethical and practical*
Encourage personal and professional target-setting				
Assign targets				
Provide incentives and rewards				
Employ escalating sanctions				
Pair the teacher with another effective colleague				
As a head, teach co-operatively with the teacher in question				
Encourage and support self-evaluation				
Send on relevant courses				
Invite external review				
Engage an external critical friend				
Appoint internal advisers/'fellows'				
Use support materials/packages				
Assign to 'easier' classes				
Reduce class size				
Reassign to learning support				
Reassign to administrative duties				
Give other duties				
Monitor closely and regularly				
Provide support in seeking other employment				
Make life difficult, increase pressure				

Appendix 4.2
Dealing with distance

Michael Schratz (Schratz and Steiner-Löffler, 1998) uses this activity to differentiate a range of attitudes among a school staff. He suggests a normal distribution with the following divisions.

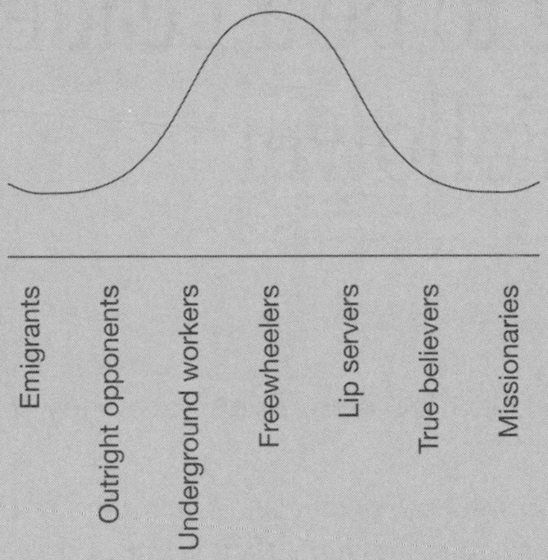

This is a practical activity that can be undertaken as a staff development exercise, during a workshop, conference or INSET.

Volunteers are asked to take up roles, for example the true believers and outright opponents. They stand about fifteen feet apart, facing one another. Their task is to convince the other person of their case (for example, the need for change in methods of teaching, the value of students evaluating teaching).

The true believer makes a statement. The outright opponent is asked to step forward if in agreement, backward if in disagreement. The size of the backward or forward step is left to the individual's strength of feeling. Remaining in place is also an option.

The outright opponent then makes a statement, perhaps a reply to the previous statement. The true believer then responds by a forward or backward step.

This may continue for five minutes or so. The audience can then be brought into the analysis of how people reach agreement or move further apart.

5

Learning to be a Leader by Being a Follower

Good leaders are excellent learners. They know how to follow and to give others their place.

> *In a learning organisation leaders may start by pursuing their own vision, but as they listen carefully to others' visions they begin to see that their own personal vision is part of something larger. This does not diminish any leader's sense of responsibility for the vision – if anything it deepens it. (Senge, 1992, p. 352)*

As we know from a substantial body of research, from our own direct experience and from the accounts of school leaders in Chapter 3, this is easier to write about than to achieve in practice. The conventional structures and life histories of schools militate against their becoming learning organisations.

All too often the place called the school is seen by headteachers as 'theirs', and it bears their imprint. It is commonplace for heads to refer to 'my school' and 'my staff' and although in some cases this may be no more than a conventional shorthand, for others it is a literal expression of how they see themselves in relation to the school. It is a tradition of long standing in British education for the headteacher to be seen as synonymous with the school and for everyone else but the head to remain anonymous. It is a powerfully entrenched tradition and has been given further impetus by the new Labour government. A DfEE press release on 3 December 1998 carried these words from the Secretary of State:

> *Good heads are the key to success. We need to develop strong leaders, reward them well and give them freedom to manage.*
>
> *Successful heads who have turned around the most challenging schools could earn up to £70,000 a year, with strengthened appraisal and the option of fixed-term contracts.*

> *We will also set up a National College for School Leadership to strengthen headship training and give it a new more dynamic focus drawing on the best that education and business can offer.*

As the person at the apex of the organisational pyramid, the head can be credited with, or held to blame for, the effectiveness and standards of the school.

The nature of the high stakes involved is reflected in media coverage of schools and their heads. Shortly preceding the Secretary of State's announcement, in November 1998, the *Birmingham Evening Mail* ran a banner headline 'School head not a failure'. It was a journalistic counterblast to the school being labelled as 'failing its pupils' by OFSTED inspectors. The paper reported that the headteacher, a 'good' and 'very experienced' head, had suffered a breakdown as a direct consequence of the report. However, his identification with the school as failing has made him a 'failing head' not only in his own eyes but also in the eyes of teachers, parents, policy-makers and the wider community.

There is both a plus and a minus to this sense of ownership. The strong identification with the school and its success is a personal driving force and powerful asset to the school. Its very power is, however, also the source of its potential weakness. When impetus is driven from above and commitment is sustained by that individual drive, the school itself may become disempowered.

Leadership is a relational concept. In other words, it carries within it an implicit notion of followers, leading logically and directly to the conclusion that the main function of leaders is to create followers. The compelling logic of the language, as Henry Mintzberg (1994) argues, may lead us straight to an erroneous conclusion – and to a practice that is inimical to personal and organisational learning.

> *What ought to be a matter for debate becomes instead structured into language with the danger that we become so enamoured of this cult of heroic leadership that we fail to see its obvious contradictions. For example, in the name of empowering the workers, we actually reinforce hierarchy. So-called empowerment becomes the empty gift of the bosses, who remain firmly in charge. (p. 80)*

Henry Mintzberg is not alone in his criticism of this model of heroic leadership, a critique now widely rejected by most management experts yet a persistent and pervasive way of seeing leadership in the British school context. In the Effective Leadership study it was the English heads who felt they were expected to be more like the heroic leader than their counterparts in other countries, in which there was a much greater emphasis on the sharing of influence and power amongst all stakeholders. In another study (Brighouse and Woods, 1999) some heads were described as 'casting such a big shadow' that it crowded out the rest of the staff.

In his research into the experience of newly appointed heads Geoff Southworth (1995) found that the experience of headship is a bit like a *déjà vu* experience, a revisiting of the initial experiences of teaching. The sense of isolation and uncertainty impels many new heads to establish themselves as strong, independent and dominant. Like the new classroom teacher, she follows the counsel to start tough and relax later because it is almost impossible to make it work the other way round. To expose yourself immediately as having a lot to learn is as risky a business for an untried head as it is for a novice class teacher. New heads and new teachers recognise that they are on trial and they know that a successful trial is one in which you convince the jury on their grounds, meeting their expectations and playing skilfully to their prejudices.

There is time later to become a learner and follower, once the terrain has been surveyed and the groundwork laid. Every new headteacher has an idea, possibly a vision, of what kind of a school she would like it to be, even if simply to maintain the *status quo*. How, over time, can that vision be realised? By maintaining a strong assertive leadership, setting out the stall from day one, leading from the front? Or can it better be achieved in the longer term by encouraging and following the leadership of others?

The answer to these questions may well depend on the stage of a school leader's career. Research by Rosenblum and colleagues (1994) in the USA found significant differences between experienced and new school principals. In the early stages the principal was often referred to as a 'visionary', an 'inspiration' and a 'change agent'. However, at a later stage, as they relaxed and matured into their job, they were more likely to be referred to as 'facilitator', 'mentor' or 'standard-bearer'. As Rosenblum concluded, this was because they were able to let go, release ownership and cede control to others. These insights find a close echo in the accounts of the 'talking heads' in Chapter 3.

While different stages place different demands on school leaders and what is effective at one stage of development may be less appropriate later on, there are, as Thomas Sergiovanni (1992) describes it, different underpinning theologies of leadership. He suggests five different ways in which headteachers may derive their authority:

- bureaucratic
- psychological
- technical–rational
- professional
- moral.

Bureaucratic authority is hierarchical, and in bureaucracies hierarchy equals perceived expertise. Those at the top know more than those at the bottom. They set standards which teachers have to reach. They enforce these through the 'expect and inspect' strategy. In-service training is provided when teachers fall short, and accountability is from bottom to top.

Psychological authority is the appliance of management wisdom. It is underpinned by working at human relations, by congeniality, by recognising people's needs and encouraging and rewarding them. The strategy is 'expect and reward'. The reward culture is an implicit statement of accountability from bottom to top.

Technical–rational authority is grounded in research, in evidence, in science. Knowing the research, being aware of good and best practice and being able to defend the position allow the head and senior management to provide the right kind of in-service support. This gives teachers the skills that have been identified by experts. Accountability is implicitly and explicitly from the bottom to those at the top.

Professional authority is where there are collective and agreed norms which are translated by teachers into professional standards. Professional knowledge is created in use, by teachers working together and sharing knowledge. Teachers recognise their mutual responsibilities to one another and hold one another accountable. They require little monitoring from the top.

Sergiovanni's final category – moral authority – derives from the explicit shared values of a community. These are not necessarily 'professional' values but those that hold a community together and of themselves guide actions and accountability. What people do is driven not by what is rewarded, or by what works, nor by self-interest. It is led by what is right and in the interests of the whole school.

Whether or not these can ever be neat discrete types, and whether or not we accept Sergiovanni's typologies, there are valuable insights to be gained from thinking about the culture of the school in relation to these five models. Perhaps the most valuable insight of all is that authority need not be located in the person of the leader but can be 'out there', in between and among people. If this can be achieved, its force is much stronger. It is mutually reinforcing. Where that shared authority is absent, psychological tricks of management come into their own and 'management' is precisely what is required to sustain the motivation. Reinforcing through reward comes into its own too where such psychological mechanisms fail, with the ultimate fall-back position being a reversion to a simple command structure.

Emile Dürkheim, the German sociologist, famously said that 'where mores are sufficient law is unnecessary, where mores are insufficient law is unenforcable'. It is a fundamental law of teaching that to lead by command is inimical to effective long-term learning. It is short-term, pragmatic at best, and carries with it a singular and indelible message about personal and institutional authority. The 'Mafia Manager' (Figure 5.1) illustrates a set of principles which directly counter those of Dürkheim, and which by virtue of their organisational origins confirm the theory that enforceable laws are likely to be short-lived.

For the teacher who has succeeded in establishing a shared set of mores, the test is to leave the classroom in the expectation that at whatever time she returns the class will be on task, working co-operatively or individually. The equivalent test of effective leadership is what happens when the headteacher or the whole senior management team are out of the school.

Where there is professional and moral authority in a school, the headteacher is freed to be a follower and a learner. Where there is professional and moral authority, it is much easier to accept disagreement and conflict. Indeed, disagreement and conflict become part of healthy organisation because people can only disagree usefully when there is an already-established ground for agreement. The improving school is one in which differences are not simply respected but engaged with, and there is a common search for meaning. David Bohm (1983), the physicist, makes the distinction between discussion (the Latin *discutio* – to tear to pieces) and the Greek *dialogos* (literally meaning flowing through it).

If you think and act solely for your own benefit you will reach the top.

'A man who wishes to make a profession of goodness in every thing must inevitably come to grief among men who are not so good. Therefore, it is necessary to learn how not to be good, and know how to use this knowledge and not use it according to the necessity of the case.' (Machiavelli, *The Prince*)

Live with wolves and you will learn how to howl.

Beginner's rules are simple:
Keep your mouth shut, your eyes open and your fly zipped, and do what you are told. Naturally, as in any business, beginners are required to kiss ass – that is, as someone once observed in another connection – you must have the morals of a whore and the manners of a dancing master – but as time goes by and you advance, these imperatives will become fewer, until finally you have become the guy presenting his cheek to be bussed.

The prudent manager will concentrate on keeping his people happily well bribed, keeping them in line, keeping them loyal and keeping the deaf, dumb and blind – in a manner of speaking of course.

When you make an example of someone make sure that everyone knows what the lesson is. Punish one, teach a hundred.

It is proper to delude others but never yourself. That is, as you work your manipulations, never become so caught up in them that you lie to yourself.

If you allow your enemies – or your friends – to think they are your equals they will immediately think they are your superiors.

If you want to be loved buy a beagle.

Most people see kindness as a weakness; because of this they welcome being told what to do in forceful terms.

Treat soldiers roughly and they will follow your orders willingly.

Be consistent, except occasionally – your inconsistency can then be used as a tactic to shake your staff out of complacency.

If you are going to walk on water you have to know where the rocks are.

Every rule is only an arbitrary border, waiting to be crossed by adventurous people. Those who would break rules may prove to be your best people.

You must set the organisation's objectives, establish a chain of command, set policies, establish controls, appraise performance, adjust and act again. In short you must manage.

In struggles for power your judgements should be based entirely on self-interest and finding as direct a route to your goal as possible.

People respond from greed; people respond out of fear. That's human nature.

Figure 5.1: Excerpts from *The Mafia Manager* by 'V' (1996)

Understanding comes first

'Seek first to understand before seeking to be understood.' This is Covey's fifth of seven hallmarks of highly effective people (Convey, 1989). He describes it in this way:

> *'Seek first to understand' involves a very deep shift in paradigm. We typically seek first to be understood. Most people do not listen with the intent to understand; they listen with the intent to reply. They're either speaking or preparing to speak. They're filtering everything through their own paradigm, reading their autobiography into other people's lives. If they have a problem with someone – a son, a spouse, an employee – their attitude is 'That person just doesn't understand'. (p. 63)*

It is a sweeping claim that 'most people do not listen with the intent to understand', but a small sample of conversation overheard on trains, in bus queues, restaurants, common rooms and staffrooms would quickly prove the statistical validity of Covey's claim. In a context where there is pressure to act and executive decisions to be made, it is doubly difficult for school leadership to listen with careful intent. Yet a genuine attempt to understand is, as Covey argues, an extremely powerful process. It is disarming both to the speaker and to the listener. It effects a paradigm shift. It can, of course, be used as a powerful technique in one's repertoire of psychological tricks. It can be employed as yet another useful management technique. In these cases it may well work in a pragmatic sense and even in a professional sense, but it will ultimately fail in a moral sense if it is not 'congruent', that is, aligned with a genuine desire to learn and to grow as a person and as a leader. Richard Paul (1996) describes the true learner as possessing these characteristics:

> *a passionate drive for clarity, fair-mindedness, a fervour for getting to the bottom of things, for listening sympathetically to opposing points of view, a compelling drive to seek out evidence, a devotion to truth as against self-interest. (p. 13)*

When we are truly learning, a fundamental change takes place, physiologically, cerebrally and emotionally. When we are *listening to learn*, we are alert, working hard, exercising the neural networks which send messages in complex patterns around the brain. This engages the logical, intuitive, emotional and memory centres which form and change our understanding. The activity, however much located inside our head, is essentially social. It is 'out there', a product of the people with whom we interact. Teachers do not 'teach' their leaders in any recognised sense of that limiting term, but they help to mediate and magnify what leaders can learn when the intellectual window of opportunity is open.

Three types of non-learning

Peter Jarvis (1997) describes different forms of confronting new knowledge, some of which he describes as non-learning. He distinguishes three types of non-learning that are as applicable to leadership as to the pupil in the classroom.

The first type of non-learning Jarvis calls 'presumption'. It may be summarised as 'I trust the world as it is known to me and I wish to maintain its fundamental validity'. To disturb the current stock of knowledge and previous learning experiences may be destabilising. It may undermine one's ability to do the job effectively on one's own terms within one's own comfort zone. This first type is 'non-learning' because it precludes change. The following statement from a deputy headteacher captures its essence:

> *She was an exciting speaker. She got everyone going and there was some heated argument among the staff following her presentation. I was unhappy she had been invited because her ideas were frankly quite seductive, if you allowed yourself to get carried away with them. I worried that it undermined the confidence of some of my colleagues in what we had committed ourselves to do as a school.*

A second type of non-learning is 'non-consideration'. This differs from the first by being an unconscious bypassing of the opportunity to learn. There's too much to do, too little time, and either learning is not seen as a priority or the potential of learning from the situation is recognised but the leader does not know how to take advantage of it. It was expressed in these terms by one departmental head:

> *In our last departmental meeting this young teacher, James, came up with this wonderful idea. To be honest I can't even now remember what it was, but I had to make a decision at the time – there is potentially something important in this for all of us. But then I lost the moment. We moved on to other business and I have just not had the time or energy to pick the idea up with James.*

A third kind of non-learning is 'rejection'. Rejection is a conscious decision not to learn because it may be seen as too difficult, too complex, too time-consuming, or too far removed from present needs to be applicable or valid. It is captured in these words from a team leader:

> *I was urged to read Perkins's book* Smart Schools. *I was finally given it as a present to* make *me read it. I started it and it was interesting enough but I couldn't really engage with it. I couldn't really see how it was going to help me in any practical way in managing my team.*

Jarvis then goes on to describe three types of reflective learning which he calls contemplation; reflective skills; and experimental learning.

Contemplation is thinking deeply, with the only source of reference oneself. In Jarvis's terminology this is 'pure thought'. In a leadership context this type might be captured by the following anecdote from a headteacher:

I often wake at about five. I sometimes find myself thinking about a situation even before I am awake. It is very relaxing to lie there and rehearse it carefully in my head, picturing it, seeing the detail of it again, seeing what I did, what I might have done, teasing out the principle, coming to understand it better. Then I get up and write it down, and find that a whole hour has passed.

The second category, reflective skills, describes a form of learning on your feet rather than in your bed. In their day-to-day work, leaders meet many situations in which they have to make rapid decisions and develop skills to meet them, sometimes in Macdonald's condition of surprise (Figure 4.1). It is important that the value of these reflective skills is recognised and added consciously and systematically to the leadership repertoire. Macdonald (1998) uses the term 'metacognition' to describe this quality of reflectiveness in action:

It would be an unremarkable statement to say that leaders in schools, as in other situations and organisations, rely upon their knowledge in making judgements and decisions. The difference between good and successful leaders and those who are less so may depend in part at least upon their awareness of the state of their knowledge. (p. 166)

Experimental learning, the third type of reflective learning, takes place when something is consciously and deliberately tried out. In a leadership context it may be a form of risk-taking in the hope that something might be learned from it, either through success or failure. The three examples that follow all stemmed from a conscious and proactive decision to follow where others might lead you.

In the first example, from a Clydebank primary school outside Glasgow, the headteacher joined in the after-school study club with the primary six and seven pupils. She said:

I achieved something I had missed for a long time as a head and something I regained by my decision to let my guard down at the after-school study club. I have been a head now for twelve years but this was the first time I had a real open adult-to-adult discussion with eleven and twelve year olds and I learned so much in the process. The relaxed environment of study club, the easy-going relationships let me drop my guard, be myself and listen to what they had to say about their lives, in the community, in the school. I think that was the first time I really began to understand, I mean really understand, what it was like to grow up in Clydebank and come to this school. And how I must appear to them normally with my guard up, and what school must be like from where they stand, or sit.

The use of the phrase 'adult-to-adult' is a provocative one. Eleven- and twelve-year-olds are not adults, yet, as the work of transactional analysts has illustrated, we all (adults and children) have three inner components to our thinking and behaving. These three components are the child, the parent and the adult. As adults, we often allow the child within us free reign. We can regress emotionally or behaviourally to a ten-year-old or five-year-old level with a little provocation, usually when someone else (an official or bureaucrat or partner) addresses us from their parent mode. Children are, in a sense, no different. They are frequently compelled to play the child role in response to the teacher or headteacher as 'parent'. However, when they play at pretend school they know how to adopt the parent role very effectively, and when treated as mature thinking beings by an 'adult-in-the-adult', they respond with the 'adult-in-the-child'.

The adult-to-adult transaction is sometimes difficult to find in the day-to-day transactions of school life. It is in the quality 'time out' which suspends the norms and releases people from their roles that this kind of adult interchange can most easily take place. It allows the headteacher to see herself in a different light, through a different lens.

The second example, from a headteacher in a secondary school, illustrates the adult–adult relationship in another 'out-of-hours' context.

> *Three lads came to see me wanting to start a guitar club. They wanted space to do it and support. They wanted to advertise it and run it themselves with a teacher to supervise. It was a spur of the moment thing but I suppose I intuitively recognised the opportunity it offered me. I volunteered to be the supervising teacher because I play the guitar myself. Badly I have to say. As the supervising teacher I had nothing to do except keep on eye on things, watch and listen. I became a regular member. They were a million miles ahead of me in guitar technique. They recognised that pretty quickly too and helped me along from where I was, not from their pinnacle of expertise. Gently but challengingly too. They were excellent teachers. They taught me so much. I think I learned a bit too about organisation and teamwork and something about pedagogy as well.*

This example illustrates something about adult learning. Its character is closer to tutoring or coaching than to teaching. In this relationship there is a greater fluidity and interchangeability of teacher and learner roles. It is a microcosm of what a school might be like if it could exceed its conventional parameters and open itself up to the possibilities of collaborative learning.

The third example is also drawn from an out-of-school context which permitted deeper learning for all. The deputy head who accompanied a Year 10–11 class on a trip to Paris said:

> *I anticipated some of the issues that would arise, issues around smoking, drinking, drugs, late nights, the temptations of Pigalle and the red light districts, red-blooded fifteen and sixteen year olds, adults or on the verge of it. I knew how futile it was to lay down the rules. I spent a lot of time before, on the journey there, over meals, in the evenings together with them exploring the issues and trying to reach an honourable and honest set of ground rules for us all. It took us into some pretty deep territory. How much I had to learn about young people's real lives. How much did I want to know? How much* should *I know? I worried that in some ways it would make my job harder next term back at school because we established such a close relationship on that trip. I was the man who knew too much. A strange concept. We*

knew more about one another than perhaps would be good for discipline, respect, drawing lines and all that. What I found when I was back at school was an immense support and no one ever crossed the formal lines that school required. They understood as well as I, if not better, how formal and informal organisations work.

It is significant, perhaps, that in all three cases it was outside the formal school day that these opportunities arose. In the adult–adult relationship pupils learned more than might have been good for discipline and distance back in the school setting. But in all three situations described there were lessons to be carried back into the mainstream of school life. Because they had been allowed to exercise their adult component, students were much more aware and more mature in their understanding of the constraints and formalities of organisational life back at school.

In all cases the experience had helped young people to recognise that headteachers are not all-knowing while pupils know nothing. These young people had learned something about the nature of learning, the nature of institutions and the character of leadership. By modelling reflective learning and followership, school leaders were able to model the quality of learning which they expected of their pupils.

In Fulfen Primary School in England there is a poster on the wall of every classroom, in the corridors and lunch room. It says 'What did you learn in school today?' The poster is aimed at pupils, asking them to reflect every day on things they have learned. Like everything else in the school environment, the poster may become all too familiar and invisible unless it is kept conspicuous and to the fore. Teachers and management need to keep the issue 'live' – by sharing with the class what *they* have learned today.

What do teachers learn in their own classrooms? Possibly very little about the subject they are teaching. The lessons they learn which stay with them for a lifetime and spill uncontrollably into their own leisure time are about human relationships, about authority, and about knowledge – its transmission and creation, and the diverse and perplexing paths it takes on the way to its destination. For good teachers – that is, reflective, critical, inquiring teachers – this is a lifelong journey and a continuously compelling one.

What does the student learn in the classroom? Something, it is hoped, about the subject they are there to study. What stays with them for a lifetime is essentially the same as for the teacher. Deeper and deeper embedded, hour by hour, day by day, week by week, is the lesson of *how* we learn individually and socially. The structure, context and tools of the classroom 'teach' where knowledge comes from, how it is made, what it is worth and how it can be used. This is more typically an unconscious than a conscious activity but, like the good teacher, the good student is able to reflect on learning itself and in so doing give shape and momentum to her thinking.

This principle must hold true for the effective headteacher. The learning opportunities are wider, more complex, and less distilled or formally mediated by another party. The sources are all around. For the headteacher who really wants to learn, the best source is perhaps the least obvious. We have a tendency to want to look elsewhere, to other schools, to other countries, to the authoritative literature, to the definitive research, to in-service courses and conferences. Yet a school and its community present immediate and abundant opportunities. These may be informal or formal, planned or unplanned. Informal ways of learning are gained through being around, by walking about, by being attuned to the spontaneous moment.

Learning by walking about is different from MBWA (management by walking about). The management walk is essentially a monitoring walk. Part of its purpose is to demonstrate the visibility of the head, a reminder of her presence, perhaps a pre-emptive strike against slackness. Its focus tends to be on predetermined things. It is a quality assurance or quality reassurance walk. The learning walk, on the other hand, anticipates surprises. It is open to seeing things differently. It is ready to spark ideas.

The difference may be highlighted by two events in two schools serving the same neighbourhood.

In school A the head is an ubiquitous presence in the school, in the corridors, in the lunch rooms, at the buses. He exchanges banter with the students and sometimes joins their table at lunchtime to talk about how they are getting on, the netball, the football team, how they are faring with their studies and with school generally. Deciding that the head might actually have wanted to hear the truth, a senior student volunteered that he found the school atmosphere 'tense' and 'oppressive'. The head turned to the three others in the group: 'That's an odd description of St J's. I'm not sure everyone would agree with you. What do you three think?' The three shrugged, laughed it off but said nothing.

In school B the head was also a constant presence around the school. He took lunch with different groups and decided to use such opportunities for a more open discussion about the school. The head sat down with a group of students, simply engaging in their conversation, disclosing a little about his job, answering a few of their questions about what other schools he had worked in and how it compared with this one. He put the question back to them. How did they think this school compared? The immediate reply was that they liked it. It was a good school. And if there was one thing you would like to change? he asked. After starting nervously with criticisms of the lunches and the attitudes of the dinner ladies the students began gradually to get the confidence, and sense the trust, to open up. The head listened quietly, nodding not necessarily in agreement but to show he had heard. Much of it he already knew. Some of it surprised him. Some of it he realised he hadn't wanted to hear. He thanked them for their honesty and said he would give it a lot of thought. He explained that some of what they said would be difficult to act on and that he didn't want to raise their expectations too high for immediate resolution, but he promised to return to them with some ideas and further questions at a later date.

Hall and Hord (1987) use the term 'one-legged conferencing' to describe this informal process through which intelligence is gathered and alliances built. The term is used to represent graphically the position adopted informally in a hallway or doorway, with knee bent and one foot resting against the wall behind. Joseph Macdonald (1989) writes about his own use of this informal learning by walking about in his role as an external critical friend to the school. His conclusions may be equally applicable to the role of the internal critical friend or school leader.

> *Those inclined to regard serious work inside the schools as a matter of achieving and applying power are unlikely to believe this. They will believe that one-legged conferencing is a weak strategy, much inferior to such strategies as formal classroom observation and critique, curriculum invention or the design of a new policy. I would argue, however, that strategies based on power relations . . . are more likely to engender destructive resistance than constructive change. The studied casualness of one-legged conferencing, on the other hand, leaves room for the perspectives of both insiders and outsiders to emerge in ways that facilitate constructive collaboration over time. (p. 209)*

The combined insights of outsiders and insiders is vital for the learning school. For school leadership the daily life of the school presents an abundance of opportunities to listen and to learn. It is salutary for anyone in a leadership position to consider how, when, where and from whom they can learn. What opportunities are there to learn:

- from teachers?
- from students?
- from parents?
- from support staff?
- from governors?

Learning leaders, says Warren Bennis (1997), 'are confident enough to recruit people better than themselves because they revel in the talents of others'. It requires a high degree of self-confidence not to be threatened by people perceived as 'better' than you, but the strength to acknowledge it is the very quality that enhances leadership in the eyes of others. People cannot fail to perceive such a strength of character, however subliminally it enters their consciousness. Leaders who see opportunities to learn from others 'walk the talk' with a very different demeanour from the monitoring supervisory walkabout.

Some heads have found the grid shown in Figure 5.2 a useful method of evaluating their learning.

Describe a recent occasion when you learned something.

From:	*About the school*	*About learning*	*About leadership*
A student or students			
A teacher or teachers			
A parent or parents			
A governor or governors			
Others			

Figure 5.2: A learning grid for heads

Learning leaders need friends

Heads may find it difficult to learn in their own school without the support of someone from outside. A critical friend with the requisite expertise and experience can be an invaluable asset, but finding the person with the right repertoire of skills is crucial. This person, or people, may be from the local authority, a university, another school, a local business person – indeed anyone who brings the insight and skills to both support and challenge effectively.

In the European Project Evaluating Quality in School Education (MacBeath *et al.*, 1999) the 101 schools were assigned, or chose, a critical friend. At the end of the project their assessment of that friend's impact was analysed and summarised in the project final report. The following were some conclusions:

- The greater the clarity and boundaries of the critical friend's role, the better the quality of collaboration.
- The facilitative role was more likely to help the school become self-directed than the more directive steering role.
- The work of the critical friend is likely to be easier and more effective where a culture of reflection and critique already exists in the school.

In the Scottish Improving School Effectiveness project (MacBeath and Mortimore, 1994) schools worked together with a critical friend whose role it was to listen carefully, to tune in to the secret harmonies of the school and to be alive to its discordances as well. Critical friends often found themselves engaging in one-legged conferencing, reaching parts it was difficult for insiders to reach. They also found themselves faced with tricky decisions about how to feed back sensitive and confidential information both to the headteacher or senior management team when such information was vital to the future welfare of the school and to them personally and professionally.

One example comes from a school in a middle-class area in the suburbs of a large British city. The school fares well in performance tables but not, in the view of the head, as well as it could, given the background of the students. The critical friend was invited in to help analyse where the school's strengths and weaknesses lay. She was given *carte blanche* to talk to staff, to students, to wander around the school, and to sit in classes for as many days as it took. At the end of day two, the critical friend had a pretty good idea of where the problems lay. She met with the headteacher at the end of the second day and reported that staff morale was low. Staff were acutely aware of divisions within the senior management team. They were less and less inclined to put in time in the school. When they talked informally the topic of conversation generally turned to the 'mismanagement team', as they were commonly referred to.

After some discussion, some denial, and an eventual concession from the head that he might be part of the problem, it was agreed to have an away-day session with the management team. The critical friend started the session by giving each member a large sheet of poster paper and asking them to draw the senior management team as they saw it. One drew the team in classic systemic analysis style, arrows back and forward describing shared jobs, communication flows, roles, responsibilities. Another member of the team drew the five members standing in a circle, each facing forward around the circle. Each held a knife buried deep into the back of the one in front – a perfect suicidal circle, as he later described it. It provoked considerable laughter but the joke had a serious purpose. The ensuing discussion helped to unearth some of the deep-lying resentments over promotions and non-promotions, credit and blame, exclusions and inclusions. There were also some deep personal hostilities and histories.

While recognising that some of the mutual dislike and resentment would remain, the team were able to see more clearly where the professional accountabilities lay and with some deep and painful learning, knew for the future how better to spot and bypass the hidden agendas and games-playing. Handling of sessions such as this requires an outsider but makes high demands on her skills and insights.

Another example from the Improving School Effectiveness study (MacBeath and Mortimore, 1995) provides some insights into the systems aspects of management and the people aspects of leadership. In that study teachers, middle managers (heads of departments) and senior managers (headteachers, deputies and assistant heads) all filled in a questionnaire with a range of common items. Data were then fed back to the schools by the critical friends, working with the staff, and sometimes parents and pupils, in sifting and interpreting the data. One of the 54 items in the questionnaire was particularly challenging for senior management in most of the schools in which it was used, carrying with it some sharp lessons for the leadership team as learners in their own school. This particular item was greeted with dismay by the head and the senior management team in one particular school. It suggested a very different set of views as to the efficacy of communication in the school (see Figure 5.3).

Percentage saying agree/strongly agree n = *65*	*Teachers*	*Middle management*	*Senior management*
There is effective communication between the senior management team and teachers	28	43	89

Figure 5.3: Response to questionnaire item by one school

The data showed a significant mismatch between the perceptions of those at the bottom, those in the middle and those at the top of the hierarchy. How could such data be explained? They could be dismissed as erroneous or irrelevant. They could be blamed on the wording and ambiguous nature of the question. They could be explained by the timing of the survey. They could, on the other hand, be seen as a vital sign, an opportunity to learn something important about communication, about the nature of the organisation, about management, about leadership and followership. In the event, senior management responded in this way:

> *This is so unfair. We have taken communication systems very seriously. We have done everything we could to put procedures in place. We circulate everything. We follow up with reminders. We raise issues at staff meetings. We ask for feedback. We check. We have a daily newsheet and a termly newsletter. I would say we are actually very good at communication.*

Why then did staff have such a pessimistic view of communication? The following comment from a teacher was also a fairly typical response and helped to explain the less sanguine view from the bottom up:

> *The management team sit at one end of the school in the management wing as it is called. Memos flow out in a pretty steady stream. There is lots of paper. Some of it I read, some of it frankly I don't. I would say they are pretty efficient but to say there is 'good' communication is another story. Good communication is not about what you say but how you say it and how you mean it. It is about the relationships in which you hear or speak.*

There is some degree of comfort for this senior management team when data from the other 35 schools in the project were listed alongside the school's own data (see Figure 5.4).

Percentage saying agree/strongly agree n = *2,605*	*Teachers*	*Middle management*	*Senior management*
There is effective communication between the senior management team and teachers	46	48	87

Figure 5.4: Response to questionnaire item by rest of schools

These national data from the 36 participating schools suggest that there might be something generic and endemic rather than specific to this one school. Indeed, the differential nature of the data appears to be a function of hierarchy and distance, often expressed symbolically in the administrative geography of the school (as in the school described above), and in the official nature of communication. The few exceptional schools that did not fit the general pattern, however, proved the rule in the most challenging of ways.

Commenting on similar exercises across a range of organisations, Margaret Wheatley (1994) comments that perceived lack of communication is a characteristic and endemic feature but not an inevitable one. It depends on how the organisation, school or otherwise, understands and responds to new insights and knowledge. Each new piece of information enters the system as 'a small fluctuation'. The leadership may choose to ignore these fluctuations, but ignoring them does not make them go away. They create a disturbance which can be allowed to take its own course or can be directed into positive energy. Wheatley (1994) concludes:

> *However long we may drag our feet, we will be forced to accept that information, freely generated and freely exchanged, is our only hope for organisations. If we fail to recognise its generative properties, we will be unable to manage in this new world. (p. 65)*

The word 'information' to which Wheatley draws our attention, is a potent reminder of the nature and structure of communication in a school where leaders are truly learners and know how to follow. The weight of evidence suggests that the support and challenge of an informed, sensitive and skilled critical friend is of immense value to a school when it comes to sifting through the difficult issues that affect the flow of its social and educational life.

This book started with examining competencies, distilled from studies of exemplary leaders. Bennis and Nanus (1985), two of the leading authors in this field, identified one competency and essential competence above all else:

> *Learning is the essential fuel for the leader, the source of high-octane energy that keeps up the energy by continually sparking new understanding, new ideas, and new challenges. It is absolutely indispensable under today's conditions of rapid change and complexity. Very simply, those who do not learn do not long survive as leaders. (p. 188)*

6

Sex, Sexism, Sexuality and Sexual Harassment

all educational leaders should be good stewards of gender and should be committed to creating positive school environments that are gender-inclusive, not simply gender-neutral. New conceptualisations of educational leadership, therefore, should embody the recognition that effective leaders are activists about gender. (Riehl and Lee, 1995, pp. 911–12)

Being an activist on matters of gender may not figure in a list of competences but is a growing imperative of leadership. The more we learn about how organisations work, and the more knowledgeable we become about the human side of management, the greater the need to take an informed pro-active stance on sex and gender.

Among school staff sex and sexuality are often treated as invisible factors or are referred to in a self-conscious way, often through jokes and innuendo. In such a climate sexual harassment can take subtle and insidious forms. It isn't always crude and overt. It is often seen (mainly by men) as just part of the give and take of relationships. Neither denial nor ritual political correctness are helpful in a context where teachers need to model an informed approach to the issues with their pupils.

For the majority of human beings sex is a given. It is decided on the basis of the reproduction functions which, for most species, are different for males and females. Gender, on the other hand, is the social ascription of sex which by definition is not given. Gender-assigned roles can differ among cultures and can change over time. Gender is not neutral but, when treated as such, can blind people to significant features of the social landscape. When this occurs in a research context it can result in misleading findings, treated as having 'scientific' validity, but resting on the assumption that gender could be treated as an insignificant variable. For example, Piaget's work on child development and Kohlberg's work on moral development were both based on research with boys. In these studies boys were seen as the norm and the findings were immediately generalised to include girls but with no evidential base for this. Gilligan (1982) subsequently demonstrated that when girls are included in such work the findings can be very different.

In organisational research and theory-building, which had also typically treated women as invisible, new insights emerged and old assumptions were challenged when experiences of women were taken into account:

> *almost inevitably, by making the invisible category of women explicit, this work has focused attention on the invisible – because – ubiquitous category of men. Thus, out of feminist or women-centred research had grown a more expansive category of gender research, which encompasses masculinity in organisational life as also problematic. (Riehl and Lee, 1995, p. 878)*

Gender, like ethnicity and class, is such a fundamental part of every individual's identity that it cannot be ignored as a factor in organisational life. The school is an arena in which children's sense of self is progressively shaped over the years, placing on teachers and headteachers a professional responsibility to be informed and to behave intelligently when it comes to matters of sex and gender.

Sex and gender

There is an ever-expanding body of literature and research on sex and gender, much of it still contested, that has contributed to demythologising and questioning of easy assumptions about innate differences. Building on the biological fact that males and females are, in some respects, essentially distinct, claims have been made about intelligence, attitudes and aptitudes for leadership. Neuroscience and evolutionary biologists make new claims on a virtually daily basis about what men and women are 'hard-wired' to do and not do, and the debate has to remain open to emerging evidence and its implications. Steven Pinker (1998), who has written extensively on the genetics of sex difference, nevertheless sees the detail of the debate as distracting from the real issues and agrees with Gloria Steinem that 'there are really not many jobs that actually require a penis or a vagina, and that all the other occupations should be open to everyone' (p. 50).

Whatever physiological, biological and genetic differences there are, they are inevitably interlinked and interwoven with the socialisation process. When specific traits are assumed by and ascribed to each sex they give that sex permission to exhibit, practise and develop them. So, for example, it may well be that because they have less testosterone than men, women are likely to be less aggressive, but it is also true that women have fewer opportunities to practise aggressive behaviour and have such conduct reinforced. On the other hand, Adler *et al.* (1993) suggest that women have more behavioural options open to them than men. They can outdo men on their own territory by being more stereotypically male than most men would wish to be and still be admired for this behaviour (a prime example of this is Margaret Thatcher), or they can be warm and approachable without being seen as violating their gender stereotype. It is much more difficult for men to imitate stereotypically female behaviour without at the same time losing status and standing. Another problem for boys and young men is that the socialisation process they are subjected to frequently denies them the opportunity to practise and develop their emotional intelligence.

Whatever innate differences are found, in most aspects of human activity there is likely to be a wider range *within* each sex than between them. For example, although the average man is taller than the average woman, the range between the tallest man and the smallest man is far greater than that between the average man and woman. Whatever generalisations are made, therefore, there will be large numbers of men and women to whom this does not apply.

Nevertheless, it is still valid to assume that, regardless of innate differences between males and females, men and women who have reached headship in the UK by the early part of the twenty-first century have on the whole been reared differently and exposed to different experiences. They also have to interact with a range of people (professionally and personally), many of whom will have different expectations of them, dependent on their gender.

These expectations can be *culture*-specific or *role*-specific.

Culture-specific expectations

> *Men may cook or weave or dress dolls or hunt hummingbirds, but if such activities are appropriate occupations of men then the whole society, men and women alike, votes them as important. When the same occupations are performed by women they are regarded as less important. (Mead, 1949)*

Cultural expectations are often based on tradition. Almost inevitably this is linked to the status of the task being considered and, of course, the reward. Throughout the world, if the task is performed by men it is likely to be seen as high status and comparatively well remunerated. The fact that there are more female doctors in the old USSR compared with the USA, for example, had more to do with status and salary (much lower in the USSR) than physiological differences between men and women.

Examples of gender-based cultural expectations are plentiful in the UK and overseas. For instance, responsibility for the market in Castries, St Lucia is solely a female province whereas in Marrakesh, Morocco the privilege belongs to the men. These expectations are not always national and can be regionally based. For example, although the number of women heads of mixed secondary schools has increased in England, there are still parts of the country where there are very few – we know of at least one northern LEA where, at the time of writing, all the secondary heads are white males.

Sometimes cultural expectations are mis-assigned to a group by outsiders based on stereotype rather than factual information. One example is provided by two schools no more than three miles apart, serving similar intakes. In one of the schools it was widely believed that there was no point in bothering too much about the education of Asian girls as they were all going to be forced into arranged marriages before school leaving age. At the other school the concern was about the over-ambition of the Asian girls who apparently all wanted to be doctors or pharmacists.

Role-specific expectations

The fact that embroidery is generally considered a female skill whereas the sewing needed for suits (tailors) and bodies (surgeons) is male has more to do with role expectations than dexterity. Lifting heavy weights is usually seen as a man's job but nursing, traditionally seen as a female occupation, is one where a capacity to lift heavy weights is important. Nurses are taught how to do this and their female 'frailties' do not seem to be problematic when they are in that role. Maintaining discipline is often believed to be better done by male teachers. Looking for a 'strong man' is not confined to the lonely hearts personal ads. It is not unknown for governing bodies to fall back on similar stereotypes when trying to fill a vacant deputy or head position.

Time and expectations

We get used to seeing men and women/girls and boys performing different tasks, but expectations can change over time. Not so long ago, indeed when Margaret Thatcher was a young MP, the idea of a woman prime minister was almost inconceivable, as was the idea that women could be directors of education (there were only two in the country) or even television newsreaders. The famous historical example cited by Franks (1999) is that of office workers who in the mid-nineteenth century were mainly male and had a relatively high status. As this changed to office workers being 98 per cent female, so did their status and remuneration. There is an interesting conundrum here, as it is not always clear whether the job in question has lower status because it is primarily associated with women or whether, because the job is of comparatively low status, women are allowed in. So were women encouraged into office work as its status changed or was it because the status changed that women started to be employed in this area? The answer of course does not have to be either/or, and almost certainly there is a feedback loop making both statements true. The important point here is that if much of what is accepted as 'the norm' is different in different parts of the world and can change over time, our stereotypes are more likely to be due to socially ascribed rather than innate differences.

Women and headship

Many writers are now suggesting that contemporary education leaders are likely to be more effective if they are less hierarchical, good at dealing with conflict, good at listening, concerned about the social and emotional development of pupils, and supportive of their staff. According to stereotypes, women should be good at these tasks. However, in 1997, women accounted for 67.3 per cent of the teaching profession but only 49.5 per cent of headships. The breakdown of women within each phase of education was as shown in Figure 6.1.

Women constitute the vast majority of the profession but they are not proportionally represented at managerial level. With regard to women aspiring to become headteachers, the picture is slightly more optimistic if registration for the (soon to be mandatory) National Professional Qualifications for Headteachers (NPQH) is anything to go by. Although still not in proportion to their numbers in the profession, more women are taking the qualification. Figure 6.2 gives details of one of the cohorts.

There are various explanations as to why we have more male than female heads. For example, men and women may have a different rationale for entering the profession in the first place.

> *Whatever the reasons, a number of studies support the notion that the motivation for entering teaching differs for men and women. Most women enter teaching to teach but most men enter teaching to administer. (Shakeshaft, 1989, p. 87)*

	Proportion of teachers (%)	*Nos*	*Proportion of heads (%)*	*Nos*
Primary	82.9	150 600	55.1	11 400
Special	67.2	9 800	41.2	500
Secondary	53.7	99 000	24.9	1 100

Figure 6.1: Women within education

(*Source*: Statistics of Education: Teachers: England and Wales 1998, DfEE.)

Note: Unfortunately statistics showing the numbers of black and ethnic minority teachers and heads have not been collected, though the TTA is now trying to rectify this.

	% of women candidates, cohort 5	*Proportion of women teachers in the profession*
Primary	72.2	82.9
Special	61.5	67.2
Secondary	43.6	53.7

Figure 6.2: Women taking NPQH
(*Source*: TTA unpublished data.)

Once in the profession, women may be less likely than men to:

- have relevant role models;
- have a career plan;
- be given appropriate experiences/opportunities in school;
- be sent on relevant inset courses, e.g. financial management/timetabling;
- have had the time to do a higher degree;
- believe they are capable of being a head (or just as important, be encouraged by someone else to believe so);
- want to move into 'management' and leave the classroom;
- be mobile;
- be willing or be able to commit the necessary time to the job.

It is of course also plausible that some appointing committees prefer to appoint men.

These are just a few possible explanations and they apply to some men too – but as can be seen from the statistics, not nearly so many. The explanations will have different weighting in the different phases. So, for example, women in primary education are more likely to have interacted with female role models than those in the special or secondary sector. Some of these explanations can be described as covert (and usually unintentional) sexual discrimination. But many women also face overt and intentional discrimination. Black women often find this compounded by racism (both covert and overt). Because there are so few of them, black and ethnic minority teachers are less likely to have had role models and may have found it harder to get the relevant whole-school experience necessary to go for promotion. This is particularly true for those who have spent large proportions of their careers involved in Section 11 work (Home Office Grant for children of new Commonwealth origins.)

Much of the list is easily rectifiable by male and female managers who can help women aspirants overcome these obstacles. So, for example, if it is true, as suggested by one of the women heads in Chapter 3, that men apply for posts when they think they can do 20 per cent of the new job, whereas women apply when the proportion is nearer 80 per cent, managers could do something about it. As well as providing opportunities and encouraging women teachers to undertake a range of experiences, they could facilitate confidence-building activities such as one-to-one coaching or mentoring from experienced female heads or inspectors they know. Several of the women interviewed in the previous chapter spoke about the support and encouragement they had received during their career from their male and female managers (heads, deputies and heads of department) and from inspectors.

Age of headship

Women tend to be appointed to their first headship later than men. In England, 37 per cent of the women heads who registered for Headlamp training (available on taking up first headship) were between the ages of 45 and 49 (compared with men, who were more likely to be between 40 and 44). A significant number of women were over 50 (18.2 per cent compared with 8.1 per cent of the men who registered). The reverse was also true, with a significant number of the men coming from a younger age group (18 per cent were aged 35–39 compared with 11.2 per cent of the women). (*Source*: unpublished TTA figures.)

Women with children may have taken career breaks and they may have waited until their children reached a certain maturity before applying for promotion. Also, many women will have taken a less direct career path than men, as illustrated in Chapter 3 (for example, trained later; moved around because of their spouse rather than for promotion purposes; or were unable to move around for promotion purposes). But applying later for headship could have as much to do with confidence and believing themselves capable of the job as anything else. It may also have some connection with all the other things they have to do outside their paid work.

Domestic responsibilities

> *How many men do what I do? I leave the school at the back of five, do the shopping make the tea, listen to the tales of woe from the kids, help the youngest with her homework then spend anything up to an hour with my older daughter who's struggling with her GCSEs. Only after that, often after nine o'clock at night I sit down to the management task I have for the following day. (Female secondary head in conversation)*

Women are more likely than men to have the sole or major responsibility for domestic life. By the time they have reached headship it is not unlikely that they will have responsibility for teenage children and an ageing parent/ parent-in-law or relative. Of course some men have these responsibilities too, but what is commonplace for women is idiosyncratic for men.

Increasingly *both* men and women resent the long hours needed to cope with professional middle-class jobs:

> *it is the professional middle classes in particular who have become the modern 'work-rich, time-poor'. Headteachers, doctors, lawyers, bankers, consultants are all affected by a long-hours culture, and all worry about the social cost. (Franks, 1999, p. 70)*

Women with childcare and/or elderly-relative-care responsibilities may not have the luxury of choice in this matter.

Being a woman head

As well as addressing these issues as a manager, some female heads still have to cope with overt and covert sexism directed at them – it does not simply stop when headship is reached. Some women find they are responsible for people (teachers and support staff) who do not want, nor in some cases believe they should, be managed by women. The resentment is not always far below the surface. Riehl and Lee (1995), for example, found that in schools with women heads, male teachers tended to rate their head less positively than did their female colleagues.

A women heads' group was formed in one London borough after a small group of newly appointed heads got so fed up with the way they were treated (chairs of governors being patronising, school keepers being rude and aggressive, delivery people assuming they were the secretary – this was particularly true for the black headteachers). The group, which started as a support group, soon expanded into training and development. For some years, with the help of the local inspectorate, they ran successful, and oversubscribed, women only courses for heads and aspiring heads. But not all women believe they need support from other women. Some who have found promotion easy and have not faced personal discrimination may find it difficult to empathise with women who have had a less fortunate experience.

Managing women

While these issues are of daily concern to many female headteachers, they are also the concern of male and female heads who manage women staff. How rife is sexism in the school? Is racism tolerated? Are these issues addressed through the curriculum and in school policies? Are there clear guidelines about what happens if a member of staff or a pupil is subjected to a sexist or racist incident? What sort of role-models are available for the pupils to learn from?

How 'family-friendly' is the school? What happens when staff want to take time off to see one of their children in a school concert or have to take time off because one of their children is ill? What happens when childcare arrangements break down and a teacher finds it difficult to stay for a meeting after school? What happens when women returning from maternity leave say they would prefer, for a temporary period, to become part-time but not lose their allowance? How are part-time staff (predominantly women) treated? For example, are they encouraged (and, where appropriate, paid) to attend meetings and INSET?

The head's main responsibility is, of course, to the pupils in her school, and any teacher absence is going to have an effect on children. But staff can be absent for a range of reasons and the kinds of reasons cited above tend only to apply to a minority. Moreover, in terms of a whole career, child-rearing years are a relatively short period. A staff who believe they are well and fairly treated are also likely to have a positive effect on children – both in and out of the classroom.

Gender differences are not just concerned with child-bearing and child-rearing responsibilities. If heads are to attempt to create and sustain a motivated workforce, it is important to be aware of the different factors that motivate women and men and to understand possible explanations for this.

In one study (Varlaam *et al.*, 1992) of over three thousand teachers (including heads and deputies) extensive differences were found between men and women teachers. Women and men rated different issues as more important for them.

> *Particularly notable differences between the sexes were noted in the proportions of men and women [with far more women suggesting] that it was very important to be kept informed about what was going on in the school, to be valued by colleagues and by management and to have a manageable level of paper work/record keeping. (p. 8)*

When asked which factors they considered unsatisfactory, men and women revealed sizeable differences. Women were more often dissatisfied with the availability of part-time work, the amount of non-contact time and the size of classes. Interestingly, in light of proposals to link performance with pay, women were not as dissatisfied with pay as men. Performance-related pay may consequently prove to be even less of an incentive for them.

Sexuality

Sexuality is a neglected aspect of organisational life, yet it is present as a constant undercurrent, part of the social processes that are linked to and underpin management/workforce relations. (Ozga and Walker, 1999)

There is a range of incidents that heads have to deal with or choose to ignore. In most schools consensual intimate relations between unmarried staff are usually not an issue these days (though in recent memory this was not the case). But heads may take a different view if the relations are adulterous and involve, for example, relationships between a member of staff and a parent. Heads have to decide if and when they have a proper concern and then what they should/can do in the circumstances. In sixth forms, 'consensual' relations can take place between a member of staff and a student, and here the waters can get very murky. The nature of 'consent' in the asymmetrical relationship of teacher and student is problematic given the power of the teacher and the 'added value' that organisational status confers. New legislation which makes this a crime punishable by a prison sentence may act as a powerful deterrent for staff, but for heads it presents a 'high-stakes' set of dilemmas.

Heads have to contend with the implications of their own sexuality as well as those of the people they manage and of the pupils in their care. Lesbian and gay heads have particular issues to face, for example, whether or not to be open about their sexuality. Many of those who make the decision to keep their personal lives private live in fear that someone will attempt to 'out' them. Uninformed (and wrong) confusions linking homosexuals to paedophiles are a particular threat for gay primary heads and teachers. Even when 'out', gay and lesbian heads know that at any time the media can zoom in on their sexuality rather than (or as well as) whatever school issue has come to their notice. The pervading homophobia of the tabloids was well illustrated by the treatment meted out to Jane Brown, a primary head in Hackney, when she came into the public eye after turning down tickets for *Romeo and Juliet*. Whatever the rights or wrongs of the issue, it was her sexuality that seemed to be of interest to the press.

While she was strongly supported by parents and local activists, exonerated by a local committee of inquiry and praised by an Office for Standards in Education (Ofsted) inspecting team, she was forced to make a humiliating public apology before national TV cameras, was attacked repeatedly in the press over a prolonged period, her privacy was invaded, she received hate mail, death threats, was physically assaulted and forced into hiding, her partner outed, her partner's children and ex-partner harassed and her work and career deeply affected. (Epstein and Johnson, 1998, p. 90)

The ethos which a head seeks to create will be all-important here. The way in which he or she behaves towards gay and lesbian teachers will be noted and discussed. Theories will be constructed on the evidence of how they respond to teachers who are 'outed', how they deal with homophobic parents or governors, or whether 'queer' is an acceptable form of pupil-to-pupil abuse in the school. Too frequently gay and lesbian adults talk about the homophobic treatment they received at school which was either not taken seriously or ignored by staff. It is very salutary that so many of them felt isolated and thought there was no teacher they could confide in (Epstein, 1994). In one study of lesbian and gay teenagers, 19 per cent had contemplated suicide (Trenchard and Warren, 1984, p. 145).

Policies that deal with these issues can be helpful, especially if they have been produced by a large group of stakeholders. But just as critical is the example set by the head. The significance of signals picked up from observing others was mentioned by several of the heads interviewed in Chapter 3 who emphasised the importance of 'modelling'. Key messages are picked up in this way.

Sexual harassment

Sexual harassment is unwanted, unwelcome and unsolicited behaviour, usually of a sexual nature or with sexual overtones, towards people in less powerful positions or circumstances (adapted from Herbert, 1992, pp. 2–3). In schools it can take place between adults; between adults and children; and between children. It is about the power of one person over another. Power in this sense does not necessarily mean formal status, so it is possible for a teacher to sexually harass his head of department and for students to harass their teacher. Sexual harassment is about trying to put someone else down – making them feel small, intimidated and power*less*. Though men and women can both be guilty of harassment, the vast majority of reported cases are males to females. This is not surprising when, in the rest of society, power is generally seen to rest with men. In schools it is not unknown for women teachers to be subjected to sexual harassment from male pupils. As both Walkerdine (1987) and Reay (1993) have demonstrated, young children can be very sexually aware, and harassment is not confined to secondary schools. Describing boys' resistance in a nursery school, Walkerdine transcribes two four-year-old boys talking to their teacher.

> *Various people on reading this transcript have commented that they are surprised and shocked to find such young children not only making explicit sexual references, but having so much power over the teacher. (p. 167)*

Reay, a former infant school teacher, described her experience as follows:

> *I have frequently felt oppressed by the boys in my charge, I have been verbally abused and, on a number of occasions, physically assaulted. At the time I rationalised that I was not a 'good enough' teacher. Since then I have seen women teachers in similar situations, challenged and upset by the aggression of a few boys in their class, and realised the problem is not of individual ineptitude, but of sexism. (p. 16)*

This type of behaviour is likely to be even more overt with older children, and can be manifested through jokey innuendoes, pointed comments about clothes and appearance (size of breasts etc.) and questions about the teacher's sex life. 'Touching up' women teachers by male pupils is also not unknown – in the classroom and in packed corridors. Needless to say, if the ethos of the school allows this sort of behaviour towards teachers to go unchecked, it is likely that female pupils will suffer more and worse. Lesbian and gay teachers and pupils are particularly vulnerable in these situations and can be at the receiving end of appaling behaviour (see for example an anonymous account in De Lyon and Migniuolo, 1989 and various accounts in Epstein, 1994).

Sexual harassment (like racial harassment) is learned behaviour and, as such, can be 'unlearned'. How the head deals with these issues is again all-important. If the head makes it clear that sexual harassment will not be tolerated in any form, adults and children are less likely to condone it and more likely to report it if it occurs. Again, his/her own behaviour towards pupils, colleagues and other adults will be noted and taken as a model.

Conclusion

In this chapter we have tried to demonstrate that sex, sexism, sexuality and sexual harassment are issues that concern schools. Ignoring them will not make them go away. Both the intended and unintended behaviour of heads with regards to these issues can have an enormous impact on the ethos of the school and the individual lives of all those connected with it.

7

Evaluating Leadership – from the Outside

> *You get the credit for everything that's right, for example a good concert, when really the teachers involved should get the credit and for everything that goes wrong, for example lost PE shorts. (Female secondary head)*

Being a head has always been seen as an important job, but recently it has become high-profile and high-stakes too. In England, there are now qualifications for aspiring heads (NPQH); financial support for in-service training for newly appointed heads (Headlamp) and courses for experienced heads (Serving Heads programme). The role of the head is seen as pivotal to the success of the school, and there are many success stories which confirm the power of the head to revitalise a school. They can no longer work behind closed doors, and it is not unusual for heads to be removed and replaced if their school receives a bad inspection report. This can mean being publicly pilloried or quietly shuffled off stage. The analogy with the company CEO or football manager is becoming less and less far-fetched as the pressure for results intensifies. The tenure of heads in English schools is more and more likely to rest on the evaluation of OFSTED inspectors.

Whereas the criteria for effective headship have in the past been largely implicit and intuitive, these are now more explicitly spelt out and judgements are made and published on the basis of those criteria. The job is increasingly open to public scrutiny, and heads have to be demonstrably and measurably effective. Getting an accurate diagnosis of the effectiveness of the leadership of a school is not, however, a simple exercise, and a range of issues have to be addressed. For a start, there has to be a dialogue about who constitutes 'the leadership' and what is meant by 'effective'. Is this different in different schools? Do staff, students, parents, LEA officials, governors, central government, have similar or different views? Whose views are important? Who needs to know?

It is important to be aware of the political context which frames the discussion and to recognise the 'philosophy', 'ideology' or set of assumptions that underpin what is often referred to as 'new public management'. Managing schools cannot be analysed and prescribed as if it occurs in a neutral, apolitical context; nor can it be evaluated in some objective, dispassionate way. More than twenty years ago Ernest House (1973) challenged the notion of objectivity in evaluation and reminded us of its inherent political purposes:

> *Contrary to common belief, evaluation is not the ultimate arbiter, delivered from our objectivity and accepted as the final judgement. Evaluation is always derived from biased origins. When someone wants to defend something or to attack something, he often evaluates it. Evaluation is a motivated behaviour. Likewise, the way in which the results of an evaluation are accepted depends on whether they help or hinder the person receiving them. Evaluation is an integral part of the political processes of our society. (p. 60)*

More recently there has been a growing critique of the common-sense claims of policy-makers who appear to believe that the process of evaluation can be somehow neutral, apolitical or objective (Gray and Wilcox, 1995; Wilcox and Gray, 1996; Ouston *et al.*, 1998; Earley, 1998). School inspection is for many teachers the single most significant evaluation of their work and is most resented when it lays claim to impartiality or objectivity. OFSTIN, the self-appointed body for monitoring standards of inspection, found:

> *a set of previously-agreed expectations and issues, which unduly influenced interpretation and judgement. Others were surprised by how quickly, and how early in the process, judgements appeared to form, and how frequently these were influenced by prior subjective expectations. (Boothroyd* et al. *1997, p. 11)*

The so-called 'new sciences' have dramatically overturned century-long beliefs about measurement, and many writers in the field of new leadership draw parallels from the worlds of the physical sciences. One of these, Margaret Wheatley (1994) comments that when we observe, whether in the sub-atomic environments or in the world of people, we participate in the creation of the reality we see.

> *If quantum matter develops a relationship with the observer and changes to meet his or her expectations, then how can there be scientific objectivity? If the scientist structures an experiment to study wave properties, then matter will behave as a wave. If the experiment is to examine particles, matter shows up in particle form. (p. 65)*

Organisational reality is similarly determined by what we pay attention to. What we see is what we look for and what we worry about is what we have decided to worry about. If we acknowledge the part we play in the process, it changes the nature of the things we talk and argue about.

Evaluation is not a simple linear process. It has many facets and manifold purposes. Among them we can distinguish an overtly political purpose, an accountability purpose, a diagnostic purpose, a formative or developmental purpose, a marketing or public relations purpose. Evaluation is, however, rarely pursued single-mindedly, but rather with a mix of intentions. The danger is that these purposes are so intertwined that whether one is a participant or the intended audience of evaluation, it is difficult to unravel the tangled skein. Consequently what is reported may be accepted without demur or, on the contrary, provokes protracted discussions of validity, reliability and applicability. Yet evaluation is critical in moving us towards a deeper understanding of leadership. A useful starting-point is the issue of audience. Who is evaluation for?

The importance of audience

In order to disentangle the various intentions of evaluation, it is important to be aware of the audience, to identify who evaluation is for and what immediate or longer-term purpose it is designed to serve. What, for example, is the purpose and primary audience for school effectiveness studies; of quality assurance reports by the local authority; of international comparisons of country-by-country performance?

One of the largest growing 'industries' in recent years is that of international comparison. The reports have a direct and highly significant impact on policy-making and far-reaching effects on the work of school leaders and classroom teachers. For example, the Third International Mathematics and Science Study (TIMMS), the OECD's education indicators, the EC's Eurydice's 'key data' on the performance of educational systems, have as their primary audience policy-makers and are explicitly designed to inform national priorities in decision-making. But in the construction and reporting of data considerable care is given to another audience, that is the media, because it is recognised that newspapers and television play a critical role in shaping public opinion and educational policy. These international studies are powerful sources of evaluation data but are rarely seen by teachers and largely unknown to school or authority leaders. Yet it is authorities, heads and teachers who are required to 'deliver' on the basis of those policies and ought, therefore, to be one of the most informed and critical of audiences.

This applies in equal measure to a form of evaluation that touches teachers more directly, that is, the school inspection report. OFSTED reports address multiple audiences, but what is their primary readership? Who are they written *for*? – the headteacher and school management team? the whole school staff? the local authority? the governors? parents? a wider public? the media? the DfEE? OFSTED itself? It would be an interesting and educational exercise to ask a group of teachers, parents, or school students to rank in order of priority the audiences which they see as the targeted readership of the OFSTED report.

Clues to audience can be found in the register, language and 'coding' of the report. The following is an example of an OFSTED report.

> *The school is outstandingly led by the headteacher, strongly supported by her senior management team and governors who are well informed about the organisation of the school. Notable strengths in leadership are the clear enunciation of the aims and purposes of the school; high expectations; the involvement of all members of the school community in decision-making and planning for improvement.*

One of the first audiences for this report was the headteacher, for whom it was a ringing personal endorsement of her efforts to take the school forward into a new era. However unwelcome an inspectorial visit was in prospect, in retrospect it was gratifying and affirming for good practice throughout the school to be so publicly recognised. It was reassuring for those parents who actually read the report and for those who became aware of it through the local press. Although the audience of this report appears on the surface to be limited to a group of local interested parties or 'stakeholders', its messages extend much wider, to the local authority, to other schools, and become assimilated into a canon of good practice. The comments on one school in fact send out more far-reaching signals and are addressed to much wider audiences. The notion of the 'beacon school' leans on this metaphor (or semaphore).

OFSTED inspections

Three aspects of OFSTED reports are worth examining in more depth if we are to understand how leadership is evaluated and if we are to gain clearer insights into what schools can do to become more expert in evaluating leadership for themselves. The three aspects we will examine in turn are:

- the content – the explicit reference points for judging effective leadership
- the medium – the style and register of reporting
- the evidential base – the transition from evidence to definitive judgement.

Matters of content

Lying behind the reporting of school, and leadership, performance lies an implicit, and increasingly explicit, view of what makes for effective schools and effective leadership. The spelling out of these in OFSTED's *New Framework for School Inspection* (1995) has been widely welcomed as it helps schools to know more clearly on what basis they are being judged.

In his Annual Report, OFSTED's Chief Inspector lists five main aspects of leadership and management. One of the five categories is simply called 'leadership', while the other four categories describe what can be inferred about leadership and management from the following: the school's ethos; implementation of school's aims, values and policies; development planning, monitoring and evaluation; and support and monitoring of teaching.

Evaluating the quality of leadership in the nation's primary schools, the Chief Inspector arrives at the judgement that three-fifths of primary schools are 'well led'. This is based on a score of 58 per cent of heads being rated in the good/very good category as giving 'clear educational direction for the school'. However, on those other four areas from which the quality of leadership is inferred, only 26 per cent are deemed good/very good on support and monitoring of teaching, 32 per cent get a good/very good grade for development planning, 53 per cent for implementation of aims and policies and 76 per cent for ethos. These gradings for different aspects of the school's 'performance' are then aggregated to arrive at a final judgement of the leadership. So, for example, management and leadership was judged to be good/very good in 50 per cent of primary schools and 56 per cent in secondary schools.

Knowing the nature of the criteria by which leadership is judged by inspectors is an important step forward and widely welcomed by senior management of schools. However, these criteria should be no more than a starting-point for a critical appraisal by school staff as to their value and relevance. Some of these features and hallmarks of effective leadership may reflect the contemporary culture and current political context. Some criteria will be suggestive rather than definitive, ephemeral rather than timeless. Some have stood the test of time while others are, no doubt, still to be invented.

Matters of language and register

Just as important as the content of reporting is the medium through which messages are relayed to a wider public. The style of OFSTED reporting has been described as 'objectivisation', in other words, categorical judgements presented as if they represented an objective reality and as if inspectors, on the basis of a one-week visit, could arrive at such definitive conclusions. OFSTED school reports have an unequivocal register. They eschew the coded language redolent of reports of years gone by which, as often as not, were likely to provoke the question – is this good or bad? The newer language and register is designed for a broader public. It is the blunt speaking that mimics the tabloid press – simple and direct. It is also quite explicitly seen as a model for other countries seeking to evolve models of accountability, quality assurance and public reporting.

The clarity, accessibility and forthright nature of school reports is in many ways a move forward. The emphasis on 'plain English' in Scottish Office documents has won them the prized quill-pen hallmark. Plain speaking and plain writing bring greater transparency to the evaluation of school performance. They help to develop a public vocabulary and perform an educative function.

What is concealed within the prose, however, is of critical relevance for how parents, teachers, pupils and the wider public evaluate schools and judge the quality of their leadership. The issue is one of 'voice'. Whose voice is being heard? How trustworthy is it? How can we know? How can we test its truth and the honesty of its intent?

Michael Fielding (1998) warns of the hidden agendas in speaking on behalf of others:

> *in speaking about others, even in the sense of describing what you take to be the case, you may, in effect, be seeking in their place, that is, speaking for them. The very language you use in your description is likely to be saturated with values, frequently your own. (p. 8)*

Quoting Alcoff, he writes:

> *In both the practice of speaking for as well as the practice of speaking about others I am engaging in the act of representing others' needs, goals, situation, and in fact* who they are. *(p. 8)*

Allowing authentic voices to emerge through the reporting of others' experience is the hallmark of good research studies, illuminating biographies and the most engaging fiction. It is what good external evaluation can do, providing an account in which people can recognise their own experience.

From observation to judgement

The third aspect of OFSTED reporting, linked closely to the other two, lies most deeply beneath the surface of what is written about school performance. What is the nature of the evidence from which inferences and conclusions are drawn? What is the reliability and validity of that evidence? What are the intermediate steps from evidence to judgement? How summative conclusions are finally arrived at is far from transparent yet is the most important and useful information for school leadership because it addresses itself to processes, relationships, expectations, ethos – the very stuff of good schools and astute leadership.

Inspectors' evaluations of leadership are subjective and based on inferential judgements by a team of people over the course of a week or so. This is true not simply of OFSTED but of many quality assurance procedures, local authority and private sector validation. Commonly they draw on four main sources of evidence: one is the self-report (explicit and inferred) by the headteacher herself; the second source is documentation – of plans, policies and communications; the third source is the direct evidence from stakeholders – teachers, pupils, parents; the fourth, observation and inference made from walking around, visiting classrooms and through informal encounters.

The first of these four sources is the head herself. Her self-presentation and behaviour over the course of the week and in pre-inspection meetings is one of the bases for judgements. For example, she presents a picture of herself through her chairing of a briefing or report-back meeting; the way in which she speaks to, listens to or includes staff in discussion; her casual encounters with staff or pupils and her apparent familiarity with them and their names; the nature of formal as well as passing discourse; how the head approaches visits to classrooms, participates in the teaching or teaches herself. Some of this is fairly open to objective analysis and description – the choice, nature and tone of language, listening skills, styles of communication and decision-making. However, this is rarely conducted in any systematic way with the kind of concern for evidence that would satisfy a research student. Many of the individual competencies, and competences, are 'picked up' through subliminal cues, things not said, body language, interpersonal chemistry.

A second source of inference on the quality of leadership is the documentation provided by the school. Qualitative judgements are made about the nature and content of the documents seen. Much of this is open to quasi-objective analysis – for example, issues of presentation, readability, language, tone. Judgements can be made about the coherence and relevance of policies, the sophistication of development plans, the level of explicit understanding of self-evaluation; and the more these judgements of 'quality' can be tied to discussible evidence, the more helpful it is for developmental purposes. While the nature of an inspection event makes it difficult to engage in such formative discourse, time and space can be created for this, and where it happens it can immeasurably enrich the process.

The third source for the quality of leadership is from other 'witnesses' who are members of the school community – teachers, pupils and parents. Some of that evidence is gathered systematically, for example through questionnaires distributed to a sample of parents, or through interviews with teachers and pupils. Again, much that is garnered is in the space between words, what is not said as much as what is said, the subtle cues for which reciprocal antennae have been trained. How these impressions and pieces of evidence come together to form a summative judgement remains to some extent a mystery. When inspectors report their findings to the school leadership, possibilities of open dialogue are constrained by the fact that they can neither reveal the sources of their data nor are able to quantify them. For example, as one headteacher reported:

> *I was frustrated by it because I couldn't tell if the criticism made of me – 'never being out of my office' – was the voice of the majority, picked up from one, two or a minority of staff, or perhaps even from a small group of pupils in a particular year group.*

The issue of voice is again to the fore. The authentic voice is inaccessible. It is mediated through the perceptions and interpretation of an inspector, or inspectors, speaking on behalf of others.

The same issues are amplified with regard to the fourth source of evidence – the organisation and ethos of the school. This can be made objective and systematic to some degree, for example, focusing on the match between planning and implementation, the congruence between policy and practice, the degree to which self-evaluation is visible and embedded in day-to-day school and classroom practice, the overall level of comfort, challenge or satisfaction as reported by people themselves. Much of the weight of judgement about effective leadership is, however, inferred from the overall climate as experienced by a visiting team. Such intuitive assessments may be highly insightful and valuable to a school, but only when they are presented in a way that can engage a dialogue and generate a concern for evidence and further inquiry.

OFSTED's Chief Inspector claimed in an off-the-cuff statement that all he needed was one day in a school to form judgements about its quality. It brought a swift rejoinder from the NUT to the effect 'Why spend a week on inspections, then?' There is a common-sense 'truth' in the Chief Inspector's remark, because some schools 'feel' comfortable and inviting while, in others, the tension is almost palpable. However, the culture, rhythms and patterns of organisational life lie much more deeply buried. They are only discernible over time, and are never static enough to be pinned down with precision. That is why inspection works best and is most positively received when feedback is given not as something definitive and objective, but as an agenda for discussion. Inspection is most effective when it offers opportunities for school leaders and inspectors together to reflect critically and openly on those deep-lying, but highly significant, aspects of school quality.

The example of the 'Beacon' school

There is a lesson about external evaluation to be learned from the development of Beacon schools. The term 'Beacon school' was designed to convey an image of shining models of good practice. The first cohort of schools was selected on the basis of OFSTED reports – exemplary schools from which others could learn. However, this was not, by and large, how Beacon schools evaluated themselves. They recognised their own strengths and weaknesses and acknowledged that it was not a matter of 'teaching' other schools, but engaging in a dialogue with them. A critical feature of that dialogue was evaluation, finding a meeting-ground for the external and internal perspectives. They did not see their role as showing off to others, but as developing collegial relationships in which there was mutual learning among networks of schools, recognising where their own strengths lay and acknowledging their own weaknesses. The suspicion, or hostility, of other non-Beacon schools was only overcome when schools presented themselves as learners and collaborators rather than models, teachers, or definitive sources of reference.

Someone who has had considerable involvement with Beacon schools is David Hargreaves, who from their very first conception has been critical of the loose terminology of 'good practice'. In common usage good practice, he argues, may be no more than a nice idea, but in order for good ideas to become validated as 'good practice' they need to be subjected to a sterner test of evidence than the judgements of an inspection team, however astute.

Jean Rudduck, addressing Beacon schools in May 1999, offered them lessons from her own study in which she illustrated the dangers of the 'grand design', the simplistic borrowing of others' practice, and the vital importance of 'contexting'. Quotes from teachers and headteachers interviewed in the course of her research illustrate these issues:

> *There is an incredible tendency in the education service to want the Grand Design – you know, this is the* huge *model that we must apply to everyone.*
>
> *There's a potential for every school to be a Beacon school in something or other.*
>
> *I feel at times there is a danger of getting to believe that the good practices are everywhere else and that the host school has got everything right and that we've got to learn from them rather than it being a two way process.*
>
> *(From address by Jean Rudduck to Beacon Schools, York, May 1999)*

These issues have a direct and significant implication for the evaluation of schools. In well-managed inspection teams much time is invested in sharing experiences, discussing and testing the basis of judgements and evidence, working closely together to ensure some commonality and consistency. In effective teams there is a recognition that judgements must be tentative and exploratory and that the nearest we can get to a valid account is by engaging in an open and searching dialogue and through a confluence of internal and external evaluation.

A Scottish example

Although different in many fundamental respects, the Scottish system shares some features with OFSTED. A four-point scale (Figure 7.1) is used to assess the quality of leadership in a range of areas, in many respects similar to those of OFSTED, but arrived at in discussion with heads and subject to prior self-evaluation by the school on the basis of 33 indicators published in the policy document *How Good is Our School?* (SOEID, 1997).

In the 1999 HM Inspectors of Schools Report, *Quality and Standards in Scottish Schools*, this was reported. 'Headteachers' leadership skills were very good or showed more strengths than weaknesses in 80% of primary and 85% of secondary schools.' Strengths singled out by HMI were:

4 =	major strengths
3 =	more strengths than weaknesses
2 =	more weaknesses than strengths
1 =	unsatisfactory

Figure 7.1: The Scottish four-point scale

- commitment and vision
- communication
- being well regarded within the school and wider community
- good working relationships and teamwork
- a supportive ethos.

Main weaknesses highlighted in primary schools were:

- too little attention to ensuring that staff followed school policies
- lack of focus on managing the curriculum
- lack of systematic monitoring of learning and teaching and feedback
- poor use of the strengths of staff in making planned improvements
- too little attention to raising pupil attainment as a main priority of the school.

Main weaknesses highlighted at secondary level were:

- not enough emphasis on focus on raising standards of achievement
- not setting high expectations for pupils' work
- not raising expectations of staff
- failure to involve senior staff more directly in monitoring the work of the school and departments.

Common to the English and Scottish models is the emphasis on policy and planning, ethos, support and monitoring of teaching, and allied to this the underpinning premise that the ultimate test of leadership is raising standards of achievement.

In Scotland an inspectorate team gathers information from a variety of sources, some formally and some informally. The education authority provides one piece of the jigsaw, forming a backdrop and set of predispositions to the judgements that will be made during the school visit. A key element in the HMI visit is the presentation by the headteacher to the visiting team. This adds a further piece to the picture being assembled, perhaps even a crucial centrepiece as it lays out the vision, the philosophy, strategy, planning, professional development and other key aspects of the school's organisational life. However, as in interviewing or public speaking it is not only the content of the presentation that is being evaluated. Also important is the effectiveness or impact, the apparent conviction the presentation carries with it, the quality of communication, its congruence with other messages being picked up by the inspectors, the headteacher's 'style'. Inspectors are expected to have keen antennae and it is the subliminal messages picked up in these interpersonal encounters that play a part in colouring and shaping their final judgement.

The inspection team will spend four hours or more in direct interview with the head (although generally less in a primary school) at different points over the week, checking out the fit between what is said and what is done.

A further important element is the systematic negotiation of inspectors' judgements with the school's senior management team. Going through the performance indicators in turn, both sides challenge the basis of evidence for judgements on a scale of 1 to 4. It is the process itself which is, again, one of the most revealing aspects of leadership. The ability of the head or senior management team to be self-critical and engage constructively in the debate tells its own story. As one inspector put it:

> *It is quite common for a headteacher to run down the list of P.I.s (performance indicators) and to say 'We have done that. We have done that. So we should get a 4.' But the very act of seeing evaluation in this mechanistic way is in itself evidence of an inadequate approach to the issue.*

At its best this collaborative pursuit of evidence tests the quality of thinking about management, leadership and effectiveness, and this forum for negotiation is seen by the Scottish Inspectorate as a seminal aspect of the quality assurance process, not only in arriving at some summative assessment but as a model in its own right for school self-evaluation.

Scottish inspectors are the first to admit to the difficulty in making categorical judgements. While a '4' (major strengths) is very often obvious and unambiguous, the borderlines between '2's and '3's and '1's and '2's is less clear-cut and more open to discussion, negotiation and a press for evidence.

The end result of the Scottish inspection may be a high commendation or an expression of serious concern about the head's ability to give appropriate leadership to the school. A grade of '1' (major weakness) may either call for an urgent and high level of support from the authority or an agreement between HMI and authority that the headteacher should be swiftly replaced, a process that it is rarely easy and never undertaken lightly. It has long been said that Scottish inspectors 'work in the spaces' and they do so usually quietly, sensitively and with respect for the incumbent rather than publicly or punitively.

Headteachers who are given a '1' or '2' in school reports are in a minority, accounting for between 5 and 15 per cent of all schools. This is, none the less, a significant proportion, and Scottish inspectors are at pains to emphasise the high-stakes nature of that assessment and the careful and scrupulous collection of evidence that needs to be gathered before final judgements are made. Scottish inspectors are also keen to emphasise that the structure of the Inspectorate, with its internal accountability, monitoring and striving for consistency, is designed to inspire confidence in the quality assurance process. Scottish inspectors bring with them a broad national experience and, by virtue of geographic scale and frequent in-service training, a consistency of approach which is not available to OFSTED-contracted teams. Self-evaluation within inspectorate teams is seen as an important modelling of what is expected of schools, and the question 'How good is our Inspectorate?' is pursued systematically along with the question 'How good is our school?'

However much the inspectorate strives for fairness and uniformity, its value will ultimately rest on the degree to which it is able to complement the school's own internal evaluation and to strengthen the capacity of the school and school leadership to be self-evaluating and self-improving. It was in recognition of this that in 1992 school self-evaluation was made a central plank of policy, and in the 1997 the new policy document *How Good is Our School?* with emphasis on the pronoun at the heart of the question signalling where the ownership of evaluation ought to lie. HGIOS, as it is known in Scotland, grew out of the good practice that had developed from the bottom up and, as that document says in its introduction, 'this came together quite naturally' – the document wrote itself.

Schools speaking for themselves

It was the experience of self-evaluation in Scotland that motivated the National Union of Teachers to commission a project aimed at developing a similar framework for schools in England and Wales. Since the publication of that study in 1996 (MacBeath *et al.*), self-evaluation has been high on the NUT policy agenda and in 1999 it co-sponsored the publication of *Schools Must Speak for Themselves*. The book (MacBeath, 1999) contains this passage:

> *There is an emerging consensus and body of wisdom about what a healthy system of school evaluation looks like. Its primary goal is to help schools to maintain and improve through critical self-reflection. It is concerned to equip teachers with the know-how to evaluate the quality of learning in their classrooms so that they do not have to rely on an external view yet welcome such a perspective because it can enhance and strengthen good practice.*
>
> *In such a system there is an important role for an Inspectorate or Office of Standards. It is to make itself as redundant as possible. It does so by seeking to reinforce the foundations of self-review and by helping schools to build more effectively on those foundations. (p. 1)*

This role of an external inspectorate is strengthened rather than diminished by strong internal evaluation. This is increasingly being acknowledged by OFSTED in their move to a 'lighter touch' and a more selective approach to inspection. In the OFSTED publication *Evaluation Matters* (1997) the Chief Inspector's introduction begins with the question 'How Good is our School?', emphasising the importance of self-evaluation. It is to that issue that we turn in the next chapter.

8

Evaluating Leadership – from the Inside

To avoid speaking on behalf of others, schools need to be able to speak for themselves. School leadership needs to have the criteria, expertise and tools for self-evaluation, to extend the scope of inquiry beyond a limited group of stakeholders and to see evaluation not as something occupying an intensive week but as extensive, internal and integral to the day-to-day life of the school.

How good is leadership in our school? The question may be answered with the same two foci taken by the Inspectorate. On the one hand, the focus could be specifically on those people who occupy formal positions of leadership within the school trying to evaluate how effective they are in carrying out their job and meeting their goals. On the other hand, the school could attempt to assess how leadership impacts on the school as a whole and is refracted through day-to-day aspects of school life.

There is a third way, and one which tends to be less addressed by external inspection. It explores the issue of leadership in a more inclusive way. It works from a wider definition. It engages in a deeper search for leadership in the myriad aspects of classroom and school life, and in shared collaborative leadership. It seeks out instances of initiative exercised by individuals and teams and looks for networks from which new leadership arise.

The school can, of course, adopt the approach that best fits the context and purposes of evaluation. In this chapter we offer some strategies. We will start with the people who hold formal positions of leadership, before moving on to examine the wider expressions of leadership.

Evaluating headship

This has two aspects: the first focuses directly on personal qualities (competencies and competences); the second infers the quality of headship from aspects of school organisation, climate and relationships.

In the 1997 version of the Scottish Office document *How Good is Our School?*, one of the 33 indicators by which schools are expected to evaluate themselves is '7.4 *Effectiveness of leadership*' (Figure 8.1). These indicators can easily be turned into a self-evaluation instrument as illustrated in Figure 8.2, allowing the headteacher to reflect on his/her performance in relation to each of the categories. This has its limitations, of course, and can be open to self-deception. The headteacher might need another perspective, perhaps that of a member of the senior management team, a head from another school, or a member of staff?

The bravest of headteachers may use this instrument in a more systematic way to get feedback from a larger sample or from a number of different viewpoints. For example, the form may be given, anonymously to:

- the senior management team
- all (or a random sample of) teachers
- the governors
- a sample of parents
- a sample of students.

It is our experience that a brave and confident head who exposes herself to this is not only prepared to see herself as others see her but will take steps to address the issues that this raises.

An instrument with a similar purpose but a somewhat different format is shown in Figures 8.3 and 8.4. This comes with two separate forms. Each carries the same items, the only difference being that one is headed 'Me as I am', while the other is headed 'Me as I would like to be'. The headteacher, or anyone else for that matter, filling out the form starts with 'Me as I am' and works down the list, scoring herself 1 to 5 on the 5-point scale. Having got to the bottom, she joins the circles to give herself a profile. She then repeats the process with an identical form, this time, however, completing the items with a focus on 'Me as I would like to be'. This gives a second, and usually quite different, profile. If the two profiles are completed on thin paper, one can then be superimposed on the other and held up to the light to see where the largest disparities lie. If they are completed on overhead transparencies or translucent sheets they can be overlaid one on top of the other. The gaps that appear illustrate the areas to be worked on as identified by the headteacher herself.

The gaps are, of course, as seen from the perspective of the individual herself and might well be different if looked at from another viewpoint. A headteacher might, therefore, wish to have another perspective – from a partner,

Performance Indicator 7.4

Effectiveness of leadership

This performance indicator is concerned with the following themes:

- professional competence and commitment;
- leadership qualities; and
- relationships with people and development of teamwork.

It refers to the headteacher of a primary, secondary or special school, the head of a secondary department or others with leadership responsibilities.

Level 4 Illustration

- He or she demonstrates a high level of professional competence and commitment based on wide-ranging up-to-date knowledge and skills, including the ability to initiate, direct, communicate, manage staff and their development and delegate effectively. Where applicable, his or her teaching is a model of good practice.
- He or she has a wide range of relevant personal qualities, including the ability to create confidence and inspire others; he or she is a positive influence on his or her area of responsibility. He or she has the ability to evaluate objectively the qualities of staff and their contributions to teamwork. He or she demonstrates breadth of vision and can take difficult decisions effectively when necessary.
- He or she has very good relationships with pupils, parents and staff. There is a planned development of teamwork, staff are involved in policy development and his or her dissemination of information is clear and prompt.

A performance broadly equivalent to that illustrated above would merit a Level 4 award.

Level 2 Illustration

- He or she demonstrates a degree of professional competence based on relevant knowledge, although this is not always successfully applied in practical contexts. There are difficulties in communicating and/or delegating effectively and attempts at initiating and directing are only partially effective. Where applicable, their teaching provides a good model in a number of respects.
- He or she demonstrates leadership but is not wholly successful in inspiring confidence in others and a number of staff do not respond to his or her management style, either because he or she is not wholly successful in inspiring confidence or does not provide a clear sense of direction. He or she lacks breadth of vision and tends to avoid difficult decisions.
- Difficulties arise at times in his or her relationships with pupils, staff and/or parents. He or she has difficulties at times in creating a team approach and while there are attempts to do so, in practice there are only occasional instances of effective teamwork and dissemination of information is not always clear or prompt.

A performance broadly equivalent to that illustrated above would merit a Level 2 award.

Figure 8.1: Effectiveness of leadership

children, or from friends or colleagues. One head who had taken the form home to be filled out by his wife, reported:

> *There wasn't a very close match between what I had done and her version of me. We had a most enlightening discussion on the subject which ended up with her saying 'Well all I can say is that you may be that person when you are in school, Harry, but that's not the person you are when you come home to me.'*

	1	2	3	4	Management? or Leadership?
Commitment					
Up-to-date knowledge					
Ability to initiate					
Ability to direct					
Communication skills					
Manages staff effectively					
Supports staff development					
Delegates effectively					
Models good teaching					
Creates confidence in others					
Inspires others					
Has a positive impact on practice					
Ability to evaluate others effectively					
Demonstrates breadth of vision					
Takes decisions effectively					
Maintains good relationships with staff					
Maintains good relationships with pupils					
Maintains good relationships with parents					
Involves others in policy development					
Disseminates information promptly and effectively					

Figure 8.2: Qualities of leadership

When people go through this exercise they very commonly say 'It depends on where and when I fill this out. I am tough in a school context but tender in the family situation. I am assertive with people in positions of power over me but deferential to those beneath me in the formal hierarchy.' In other words, these are not fixed competences but personal qualities which may express themselves differently in different contexts. It again underlines the point made in Chapters 2 and 3 that we are, in fact, different people in different contexts and within different relationships. The headteacher in Chapter 3 who described herself as 'compassionate, gentle and thoughtful' but also 'strategic, innovative and astute', recognised the importance of context in determining how she would behave and, in a sense, who she was.

It is a virtue rather than a flaw of a self-evaluation protocol such as this that it is context-dependent. When the exercise is engaged with in a professional development context, therefore, it can provide an excellent tin-opener, disclosing issues

rule breaker	1	2	3	4	5	rule observer
efficient	1	2	3	4	5	inefficient
radical	1	2	3	4	5	conservative
share power	1	2	3	4	5	hold power
authoritarian	1	2	3	4	5	democratic
charismatic	1	2	3	4	5	reserved
pursue long-term goals	1	2	3	4	5	pursue short-term goals
forgiving	1	2	3	4	5	unforgiving
competitive	1	2	3	4	5	uncompetitive
delegate a lot	1	2	3	4	5	delegate very little
like change	1	2	3	4	5	dislike change
confront bad practice	1	2	3	4	5	tolerate bad practice
gentle	1	2	3	4	5	tough
reliable	1	2	3	4	5	erratic
strong values	1	2	3	4	5	open-minded
attend to detail	1	2	3	4	5	careless about detail
gregarious	1	2	3	4	5	private
size up people well	1	2	3	4	5	bad at sizing up people
demanding	1	2	3	4	5	undemanding
individualistic	1	2	3	4	5	team player
inflexible	1	2	3	4	5	flexible
optimist	1	2	3	4	5	pessimist
fight for beliefs	1	2	3	4	5	back off from a fight
entrepreneurial	1	2	3	4	5	cautious
predictable	1	2	3	4	5	unpredictable
take risks	1	2	3	4	5	avoid risks
take decisions easily	1	2	3	4	5	difficulty in decision-making
assertive	1	2	3	4	5	unassertive
manipulative	1	2	3	4	5	straightforward
easily influenced	1	2	3	4	5	unbending
low profile	1	2	3	4	5	high profile
idealistic	1	2	3	4	5	pragmatic
listen more than talk	1	2	3	4	5	talk more than listen
lead from the front	1	2	3	4	5	lead from the back
....	1	2	3	4	5	....

Figure 8.3: Me as I am

for wider discussion within the group. The exercise can be undertaken explicitly with reference to specific contexts or time of the year, week or day, for example:

Me as I am:

- in management team meetings
- in whole-staff meetings
- leading training sessions
- observing teaching in classrooms
- conducting appraisals
- engaging in an OFSTED inspection
- at an informal staff function
- at a local authority conference.

rule breaker	1	2	3	4	5	rule observer
efficient	1	2	3	4	5	inefficient
radical	1	2	3	4	5	conservative
share power	1	2	3	4	5	hold power
authoritarian	1	2	3	4	5	democratic
charismatic	1	2	3	4	5	reserved
forgiving	1	2	3	4	5	unforgiving
competitive	1	2	3	4	5	uncompetitive
delegate a lot	1	2	3	4	5	delegate very little
like change	1	2	3	4	5	dislike change
confront bad practice	1	2	3	4	5	tolerate bad practice
gentle	1	2	3	4	5	tough
reliable	1	2	3	4	5	erratic
strong values	1	2	3	4	5	open-minded
attend to detail	1	2	3	4	5	careless about detail
gregarious	1	2	3	4	5	private
size up people well	1	2	3	4	5	bad at sizing up people
demanding	1	2	3	4	5	undemanding
individualistic	1	2	3	4	5	team player
inflexible	1	2	3	4	5	flexible
optimist	1	2	3	4	5	pessimist
fight for beliefs	1	2	3	4	5	back off from a fight
entrepreneurial	1	2	3	4	5	cautious
predictable	1	2	3	4	5	unpredictable
pursue long-term goals	1	2	3	4	5	pursue short-term goals
take risks	1	2	3	4	5	avoid risks
take decisions easily	1	2	3	4	5	difficulty in decision-making
assertive	1	2	3	4	5	unassertive
manipulative	1	2	3	4	5	straightforward
easily influenced	1	2	3	4	5	unbending
low profile	1	2	3	4	5	high profile
idealistic	1	2	3	4	5	pragmatic
listen more than talk	1	2	3	4	5	talk more than listen
lead from the front	1	2	3	4	5	lead from the back
....	1	2	3	4	5	....

Figure 8.4: Me as I would like to be

The more we move away from static competences to more fluid contextual behaviour, the more useful the evaluation instrument becomes as a diagnostic or formative tool. If we can find simple tools that combine Jerome Bruner's twin principles of economy and power, insights to be gained can have an immediacy and spontaneity without losing the cutting-edge that effective evaluation requires.

The simple pie chart in Figure 8.5 exemplifies economy taken to its most pristine form, but is also a relatively powerful device. The headteacher is asked to make an intuitive judgement about her management style. What is the balance among command, consultation and consensus? The 'talking heads' in Chapter 3 who described their style would have responded to this very differently, some with a fairly high degree of command, all with a large degree of consultation and at least one with a virtually full circle on consensus.

In the example shown in Figure 8.5 the headteacher sees herself primarily as consultative, seeking consensus much of the time and only occasionally in the command mode.

The economy of this instrument, some might say, is too simplistic by half, but its real power comes when used with others, asking for their judgements of how decisions come to be made in the organisation. Figure 8.6 gives three different versions from the same school, except that it is clearly not the 'same' school for its different members.

While the differences of perception which this instrument can engender may lead to useful and challenging debate, it provides an opportunity to go beyond opinion and counter-opinion with a more rigorous analysis. It can be a first step in clarifying the language of the 'three Cs'. What is 'consultation' to me may not be consultation from where you stand. What I see as 'consensus' may be for you majority vote, or even thinly disguised 'command'. Evaluation can then move beyond this to look, for example, at recent crunch decisions, which can be revisited and unpacked again. Or it can focus on a decision about to be made (say, over the forthcoming week), so providing a prospective, rather than a retrospective, record. Analysis might be undertaken by the headteacher herself, primarily for her own enlightenment, or it may be undertaken with the management team as a whole or, with still more risk attached, involving a whole staff or small representative group of staff.

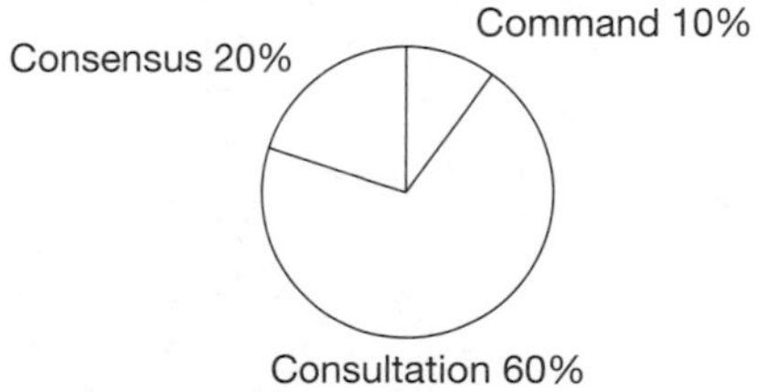

Figure 8.5: Command, consensus and control

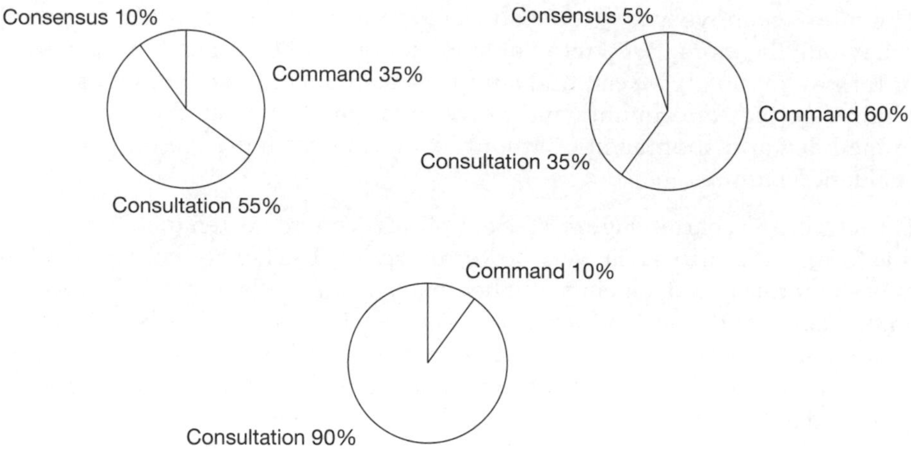

Figure 8.6: Command, consensus and control from three different perspectives

Values and time

Another fairly economical but potentially powerful device is the one-day diary. It was used to great effect in the Effective Leadership study, not only from the point of view of generating interesting research data but for the revelations it provided for the participating heads themselves. The researchers asked heads to think about what was important to them and to prioritise these values, say in order from 1 to 7. They were then asked to keep a detailed diary over the course of just one day, noting actions – where they took place, with whom, with what outcome, with what purpose. The completed diaries were then set alongside the value priority list to examine the closeness of fit (see Figure 8.7).

Values	Time
What is most important to: • Me? • The school?	• What? • Who with? • Where? • With what outcome? • With what purpose?

Figure 8.7: Values and time

This proved to be both a confirming as well as a challenging exercise. Headteachers were, on the whole, relieved and pleased to find a fairly close match between the values they professed and the time they invested, but this was not always the case, and the mismatch between intention and actuality was not only thought-provoking but led to some hard-headed discussion about how to bring these into closer conjunction.

The four quadrants

A companion exercise which might help to move insights a little closer towards action is the urgency/importance matrix. It is familiar to many headteachers as a staple on management courses. It is sometimes dismissed as irrelevant in a school context of constant surprise and unpredictability. It can, however, be very useful as a starting-point for examining values and action or as a sequel to the values/diary exercise. The four quadrants shown in Figure 8.8 allow headteachers (or other members of the school community) to put tasks, events and actions into whichever of the four quadrants is most appropriate. Every letter, phone call, memo, interview or visit in a given period of time is recorded in one of these categories.

Stephen Covey (1989), the chief advocate of this tool, argues that the large bulk of leaders' time should be in quadrant 2. Where this isn't the case, he suggests, it is a time for some reflection, replanning and intensive review. He describes the four quadrants as in Figure 8.9.

As a developmental tool this can be used at any level from the classroom teacher to pupils organising their leisure, study and personal lives.

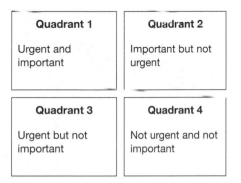

Quadrant 1 Urgent and important	**Quadrant 2** Important but not urgent
Quadrant 3 Urgent but not important	**Quadrant 4** Not urgent and not important

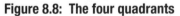

Figure 8.8: The four quadrants

Quadrant 1	Quadrant 2
Crises Pressing problems Deadline-driven projects and meetings	Preparation Prevention Values clarification Relationship building Empowerment Relaxation
Needless interruptions Unimportant meetings, phone calls Other people's minor issues	Trivia, busywork Time wasters Escape activities Irrelevant mail Excessive relaxation
Quadrant 3	**Quadrant 4**

Figure 8.9

Sketches of leadership

Another economical and powerful device used in the Effective Leadership study was the freehand spontaneous drawing of leadership as seen from a number of perspectives. At the start of the project, participating headteachers were given the freedom of a large A2 sheet of paper to depict themselves in relation to their job. Figures 8.10(a) and (b) give two examples of those art

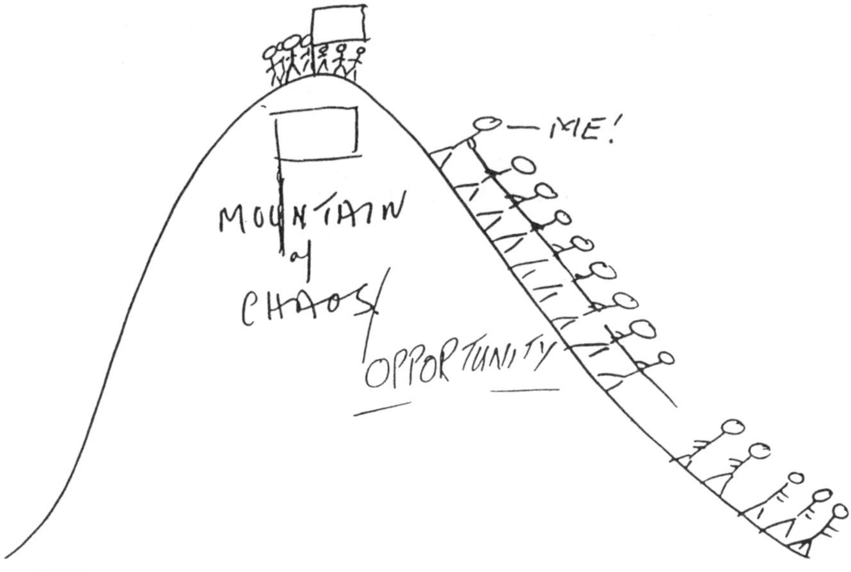

Figure 8.10a

Figure 8.10b

works. Their illustrations sparked extended and significant discussion, so much so that the research team later published the taped record of these, together with drawings, as *Images of Leadership* (MacBeath *et al.*, 1994).

The second stage of the exercise was to go through a similar exercise from a pupil viewpoint. This produced a range of colourful and sometimes idiosyncratic views of headteachers. Examples of these are illustrated in Figures 8.11(a) to (d).

The card sort

Another device used in the Effective Leadership study was the card sort. After some discussion and piloting with different stakeholder groups, a set of cards was devised, each card bearing one statement about the role or possible functions of the headteacher. Groups (pupils, parents, teachers) were then asked to lay the cards out in front of them on the table and, as a group, to agree on the most and least important ones and arrange them in order of priority.

Figure 8.11a: What does a Headteacher do?

Figure 8.11b

The headteacher visits classrooms and says 'well done' to the boys and girls

Figure 8.11c

The headteacher stays behind after school and dances in the hall

Figure 8.11d

Another approach to prioritising used in the same project was a more conventional one, a five-category response sheet asking people (governors, parents, teachers) to choose their most and least preferred models of leadership. The differences within and between groups led to rich and useful debate in return for a very small investment of time. A copy of this instrument is shown in Figure 8.12.

The critical-friend interview

In Chapter 6 the role and functions of the critical friend in supporting self-evaluation are described. In the European Project *Evaluating Quality in School*

Which of the following five definitions of leadership is the closest to your own view? Please put a tick (✓) in the appropriate box.

Which of the above five definitions of leadership is furthest away from your own view? Please put a cross (✗) in the appropriate box.

	Leadership means having a clear personal vision of what you want to achieve, a commitment to a set of deeply held set of values and principles, and the ability to inspire people and take them with you.	
	Good leaders are in the thick of things, working alongside their colleagues, sharing power, demonstrating a capacity to learn as well as to lead by example, encouraging the leadership of others.	
	Leadership in a school context means respecting the autonomy and professionalism of the individual teacher, protecting him/her from extraneous demands, allowing him/her to be effective in the classroom.	
	Good leaders have the capacity to look ahead, to anticipate change, to prepare people for it so that it does not surprise or disempower them. They create a climate in which change is seen as challenging and professionally invigorating.	
	Good leaders are pragmatic. They are able to grasp the realities of the political and economic context. They know how to negotiate and when to compromise and how to get the best out of the system for the benefit of their own school.	

Figure 8.12: The meaning of leadership

Education (MacBeath *et al.*, 1999), it was seen by schools as the most valuable ingredient in helping them to become more aware, critical and self-improving. Critical friends were outside consultants – industrialists, university lecturers, board members, or sometimes parents – allocated to the school (or chosen by them) to work with teachers, the management team or with the headteacher specifically. Their role was to be both supportive and challenging. In one of the Finnish schools in the project the head described her relationship with the critical friend as of one of the most difficult but fruitful episodes of her 32-year career. Her critical friend had cleared an afternoon with her, then started the interview off with the request 'Tell me about your job.' The session lasted four hours and although the critical friend spoke very little she helped her, in the headteacher's words, 'travel a path I had never travelled before'.

The critical friend can play a valuable role in supporting the process of self-evaluation, offering the challenge to complacent, uncritical, or over-generous self-assessment. This may be through the kind of open-ended interview described or by using some of the self-assessment tools as a focus for the dialogue. The critical-friend role is one that can affirm, surprise, and reveal unrecognised depths and unsuspected assets. It is a sensitive and complex role about which comparatively little has been written. The range of skills described by heads who had evaluated the impact of the critical friend in the European Project is shown in Figure 8.13.

Collegial consultancy

Collegial consultancy can provide a different kind of in-depth evaluation. It may take many different forms, but the one that follows has proved itself in a range of different contexts. It works as now described.

Anything from five to fifteen leaders form a circle. One has volunteered beforehand to prepare a five- to ten-minute talk on a challenge she is currently facing. She starts by sketching the background of her school. She then goes on to describe how she sees the issue she is currently wrestling with. The task of the group is to listen as sensitively and accurately as possible so that they can follow up with intelligent and probing questions. The essential elements of the protocol are:

- seek first to understand
- try to get inside the issue from the speaker's standpoint
- ask questions that are designed to help her think through the issues
- don't preach
- don't anecdotalise
- don't offer suggestions as to what you did in your school.

Role	*Skills*
Adviser	• provides useful advice • offers a clear picture of the school's strong and weak points • gives information and materials about self-evaluation and development planning • suggests methods and other forms of support • gives clear guidelines on how to implement proposals.
Organiser	• moderates meetings • keeps time • structures the process • helps organise the work • provides guidelines for actions • prepares meetings or whole school activities • comments on strategic discussions • sets out clear objectives • directs working parties effectively.
Motivator	• gives reassurance and encouragement • is a good listener • gives reassurance and encouragement • creates a sense of importance of the project in the school • demands more from the school • is inspiring and encouraging • stops people from becoming too ambitious • makes self-evaluation understandable • helps in finding new ideas • keeps the work going • proceeds by small steps • gives an idea of where thing lead to • promotes ongoing activities • helps bridge gaps • helps in focusing • encourages a positive approach to collaborative work • helps to motivate the pupils and parents to co-operate in the project • prompts the action groups to recast the working tools.
Facilitator	• handles emotions • keeps the balance between personal and professional matters • lays fresh emphasis on the context-related aspects of the learning process at school • asks questions about interpersonal relations.
Networker	• builds networks • suggests possible partners outside/from other schools • helps in team-building • strengthens the co-operation between school and work • acts as a contact person with students of the teacher training college and the university.
Outsider	• brings in an outside view • is critical of the 'ordinary' • occasionally brings in counter arguments • creates multiple perspectives • mirrors one's own perceptions • enhances coherence among diverse viewpoints • calls the school into question in terms of its organisational aspects • analyses the school having the perspective of another enterprise.

Figure 8.13: The roles and skills of the critical friend

While this process does not preclude advice, it tends to be given or asked for only after the speaker's context has been grasped by the group and then offered in the form of 'Have you thought of . . .?', 'have you tried. . .?'

The technique was used to great advantage in the context of a seven-country study by the Bertelsmann Foundation. In one session a Dutch school leader talked about her difficulties in getting the teaching staff to change their life-time-ingrained habits. When it came to the 'Have you tried/have you thought of . . .?' questions her answers were 'Yes, we've done that. Yes, we have a school council. We have a newsletter. Yes, we do have praise systems for students. We have working parties. Yes, we have a mission statement, a school development plan, a system of review. Yes, we have staff appraisal.' Thirty-five minutes into the session a group member remarked, 'You seem to have everything. Yet I get a sense you have nothing.' This struck a chord with the headteacher in the hot seat. She didn't reply immediately but wrote silently. In the fifteen seconds or so of silence that ensued within the group the true nature of the issue was being grasped. It was eventually articulated by another head who said:

> *It has brought something home to me. I have got the structures but never really deeply tackled the culture issue. In fact the more I think about this the more I see the structures as an impediment, not a support.*

In these sessions the last five to ten minutes are given over to reflection on what has been learned by the participants. Each participant in turn says one thing that they have learned until finally it is the turn of the incumbent of the hot seat to reflect on what she has gained from the session. Articulating this and sharing it with the group, which has been through a common experience, proves to be an important part of the summary and closure of the session. In our experience a session like this can easily last for an hour and a half or more. It is an important aspect of planning to allow that kind of space and time so that the session can develop its own equilibrium and its own momentum.

These sessions have a special quality, a thoughtful, unhurried, reflective ethos. At the end of the session described above, a Norwegian headteacher, summarising what she had learned, said:

> *For me it was like turning the pages of a book. With each page we moved deeper and deeper into the heart of the story. The mystery deepened. But as we got deeper and deeper the mystery also began to unravel. We began to see the light and find a happy ending.*

This in-depth analysis often crosses the threshold from evaluating the individuals in formal leadership positions to leadership as expressed through the culture and character of the school. Leadership comes to be seen as a moving, restless, dynamic process. The quality of leadership is refracted through the facets and fragments of school life. It is seen in the corridor traffic, the entry and exits from classes, to brief encounters in hallways and on staircases, in the rhythm of classroom life and the harmonies of relationship.

Evaluating shared leadership

In evaluating leadership through the organisation and ethos of the school we might ask questions such as these:

- Where does the school get its energy from?
- Is there a sense of purpose and direction?
- Where and from whom does that sense come?
- How are decisions made?
- Where are the networks?
- What are the shared norms?
- How do norms change over time?

When we ask these kinds of questions and probe carefully for the answers, we will probably arrive at a highly complex view of how change, power and authority work. These questions unveil informal status, assumed rather than conferred. They illuminate shared vision and authority, emergent decision-making, currents and cross-currents of influence, push and pull, public and private authority, high-profile vacuity and low-profile effectiveness. Answers to these questions may reveal the nature of informal networks and their significance in sustaining people in times of pressure and stress.

When we change the focus from the person of the headteacher to the ethos of the school we can revisit some of the tools described earlier but with a different focus. We may, for example, reframe the 'Me as I am' instrument to become an organisational probe. It might look something like Figure 8.14. This may be used to help dig a little deeper into those subjective but none the less significant impressions, the 'feel' of the school. The dialogue that it stimulates can lead deeper and deeper into an examination of what lies beneath those surface characteristics of school ethos.

Development analysis interview

The development analysis interview has been used by researchers to explore the school's capacity for change. In this particular model researchers conduct two-handed interviews, with the headteacher and someone else in the school who brought a different perspective on recent developments. The two interviewees are asked to focus on a change or development that the school has been through in the last year or more. The task of the interviewer is to lead them back through the change process in careful detail, eliciting not only what was done and by whom, but the intentions, feelings and impact of the change. A substantial amount of qualitative data can be accumulated from such an interview, lasting up to an hour and a half. The task of the interviewer, or criti-

tidy	1	2	3	4	5	untidy
warm	1	2	3	4	5	cold
parent-friendly	1	2	3	4	5	parent-unfriendly
colourful	1	2	3	4	5	drab
authoritarian	1	2	3	4	5	democratic
comfortable	1	2	3	4	5	uncomfortable
orderly	1	2	3	4	5	disorderly
sensitive	1	2	3	4	5	insensitive
strict	1	2	3	4	5	easy-going
high stress	1	2	3	4	5	low stress
pessimistic	1	2	3	4	5	optimistic
tense	1	2	3	4	5	relaxed
helpful	1	2	3	4	5	unhelpful
competitive	1	2	3	4	5	uncompetitive
formal	1	2	3	4	5	informal
reactive	1	2	3	4	5	proactive
likes change	1	2	3	4	5	dislikes change
stimulating	1	2	3	4	5	boring
pupil-friendly	1	2	3	4	5	pupil-unfriendly
inflexible	1	2	3	4	5	flexible
clear values	1	2	3	4	5	no clear values
avoids conflict	1	2	3	4	5	responds well to conflict
adventurous	1	2	3	4	5	cautious
uses time well	1	2	3	4	5	time used badly
risk-taking	1	2	3	4	5	avoids risks
open to new ideas	1	2	3	4	5	sceptical of new ideas
idealistic	1	2	3	4	5	pragmatic
pursues long-term goals	1	2	3	4	5	pursues short-term goals
looks to the past	1	2	3	4	5	looks to the future
…………………	1	2	3	4	5	…………………

Figure 8.14: Ethos indicators

cal friend, is then to categorise and 'score' these data to give a judgement of the school's capacity to handle change. So, on the basis of how the two significant actors in the school conceptualise change, inferences can be made as to whether the development is seen as reactive or proactive, simplistic or sophisticated, or revealing a capacity for self-reflection and self-improvement.

The interviewer or critical friend has to come to the exercise with objectivity and critical distance, and school staff need to be prepared for a level of analysis and feedback that is highly challenging.

The quadrant

The matrix in Figure 8.15 is one that has been used by commercial companies to categorise their employees on two intersecting scales – positive to negative and high to low energy.

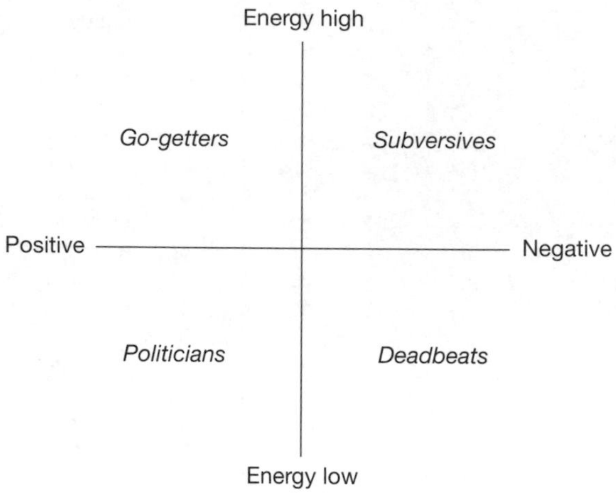

Figure 8.15: Evaluating staff – energy and attitude

It isn't difficult for headteachers to start writing names of their staff into the four quadrants. To put people into boxes like this does, however, rest on two assumptions: (1) that the vantage-point – your own as a headteacher – provides a good or accurate view of the terrain; (2) that qualities – of energy and positivity – actually belong to the individuals, that they are inherent and fixed.

It is instructive, therefore, to test these two assumptions. One way is by changing the viewpoint or viewer. The same instrument in the hands of a fellow trade union member, the secretary of the angling club, a fellow football supporter, or someone's children might give a very different picture of energy and positivity. Within the school context we might test some of the assumptions of the 'human qualities' models by focusing on the context and conditions which create go-getters out of deadbeats, which allow politicians to find new energy and encourage subversives to channel their energies into new constructive outlets. The following is one way in which this can be used as a staff development activity.

Think back over the last term of school. Now think of times, places, relationships in which you were highly positive and full of energy. Write them in quadrant 1.

Now think of times when you felt like a real deadbeat, negative and devoid of energy. Write them in quadrant 4.

Now think of times when you had a strong negative feeling (for example, about the school or the authority or the government) and were so energised by it that you took some action (a complaint, a letter, a phone call). Write these in quadrant 2.

Now think of times when you felt no enthusiasm or energy for what was going on but put a good face on it, accepted or even endorsed something for the sake of a quiet life. Write these in quadrant 3.

As a development exercise this can help everyone to reflect on the school as an energy system, producing or draining off energy in different places, at different times of the year, and depending on the ebb and flow of relationships. Understanding the ecosystem of the school tells its own story about contexts of leadership. To what extent are these places created and recreated by effective leadership? To what extent do they have a life and momentum of their own? As a self-evaluation tool the quadrant exercise can lend insights into the organisational life of the school and help to spotlight what might be changed for the better.

Photo-evaluation

A thermal imaging camera would be able to capture the hotspots and cold blue places in the school's energy system, showing where energy is created and entropy doing its dirty work. Taking photographs is the closest we can approximate to this, but may offer some more far-reaching insights than the high-tech equivalent. The headteacher of a Scottish primary school, Susan Ross (1995) describes what she did to involve parents in the evaluation of their school through the use of this approach.

> *A further opportunity to extend the discussion with parents was offered by the decision to photograph 'a day in the life of Coalsnaughton Primary'. John MacBeath, who was still working with the school, acted as the proverbial 'eye' for the course of one day, providing a collection of photographs which gave a comprehensive insight into the ethos of the school.*
>
> *Here was visual evidence of relationships, pupil–pupil and teacher–pupil, giving us another focus to assess the ethos of the school and to deepen discussion on the school's main purposes and values. What did the photos say about the ethos we were trying to create? How could that ethos support and enhance pupils' ability to learn? A second parents' evening was held. With the questionnaire results as a backdrop to discussion, parents were asked to work in small groups, listing all the things they thought made a 'good' school. They then had to select and agree on ten. Their next task was to look through the photographs and see if they could find evidence in Coalsnaughton school to match their criteria of a 'good' school. (p. 28)*

Two Austrian researchers, Ulrike Steiner-Löffler and Michael Schratz (1996) have extended the use of this technique. They give cameras to groups of students, inviting them to plan together and then, on camera, to capture places, people, events that to them say something significant about the school, whether in terms of physical provision, ethos, or teaching and learning.

One of the photographs they cite as an example is the closed door to the headteacher's study. They ask, 'From a student perspective, what messages are being sent out from that inanimate object? What kind of energy system lies behind that door?' When discussion is embarked on with students, familiar places become invested with new meaning – the head's office is no longer the administrative centre of the school, but seen as a door behind which dangers lurk. The staffroom is seen, not as teachers see it, a retreat, a respite centre, but as 'the place where boring lessons come from'.

Diaries and logs

Headteachers, teachers and students often keep diaries on an informal and voluntary basis but the 'log' or diary can be put to systematic use to focus on an aspect of the school at a given time or with a specific theme. The homework log is an example of record-keeping that has been used to give an insight into what happens when students are left on their own to do their homework or study.

The approach is quite simple. A class or year group is asked to keep a careful record over the space of a week of what they did from the time of arriving home until bedtime and for the whole day on Saturday and Sunday. Carried out in a climate of trust and honest 'research', this has a number of benefits. It provides a view for students themselves of how they divide their time and how effective they are in using their time and resources. The greater value comes from the process of sharing and discussing the data in groups, with teachers, team leaders and senior management. It can be a useful tool for making homework or study more efficient and effective but, like all good tools, it can be put to other purposes such as classroom and school-wide learning.

Spot checks

The spot check is a way of ascertaining, at a given moment during the lesson, what is happening. It is in a sense like lifting a single frame from a moving picture at a totally arbitrary moment. One simple, easy-to-use version of this is for the teacher to stand back from the lesson and ask three questions:

- What are the students doing?
- What are they learning?
- What am I doing?

To this may be added a fourth, formative, question: 'What am I going to do next?' This exercise is obviously best undertaken when students are engaged in some activity and the teacher is free to observe. The answer to the question

'What are they doing?' may have a simple reply – writing in their books. But a little deeper probing might reveal some more complex and varied activity – some writing, some copying from their neighbour, some stuck and looking for help. The deeper question, 'What are they learning?' might require a sampling of the quality of work or some questioning of an individual student. When teachers do this they are sometimes shocked to find the misconceptions that students are working on and the lack of any deeper level of understanding.

A study in Singapore classrooms (Tay-Koay Seiw Luan, 1997), in which students in their final year of secondary school were asked to report about their thinking during a lesson, revealed the data shown in Figure 8.16, disaggregated by the ability of the student.

Probing still further into their learning processes, students were asked what was actually going on in their minds during a lesson, in an attempt to identify the intellectual skills that were being exercised. See Figure 8.17 for the findings.

These kinds of results were repeated across a number of different observed lessons. They paint a disappointing picture for a country at the apex of international league tables of attainment, but not an unexpected one. Headlines in Singapore's *Straits Times* about 'the overtaught Singapore student' and calls for a deep cut in curriculum content are a response to growing evidence from employers and universities that students have acquired exam-passing skills at the expense of thinking skills and aptitudes for lifelong learning.

As a self-evaluation tool, a spot-check instrument, which asks students to reflect on their thinking, can offer to both teacher and pupil insights into the quality of learning as well as a conceptual vocabulary to raise awareness of metacognitive skills – thinking about how we are thinking. Self-reporting of this nature requires of students some high-level language skills as well as conceptual skills, but it is a way of introducing them to a higher level of self-analysis, or 'metacognitive' activity. For teachers to use in their own classrooms to help students monitor their own learning strategies, it can be an invaluable development tool.

	Low ability	*Average ability*	*High ability*
Not thinking actively	29	16	14
Lesson-irrelevant thinking	26	23	33
Lesson-relevant thinking	36	45	30
Lesson-relevant and -irrelevant thinking	9	16	24

Figure 8.16: What were they thinking
(*Source*: Tay-Koay Seiw Luan, 1997.)

What pupils were doing	*% of pupils self-report on lesson*
Note taking	21
Responding to questions	9
Trying to understand	45
Visualising	6
Assimilating	7
Applying	1
Hypothesising	2
Analysing	5
Evaluating	3

Figure 8.17: What were they doing?
(*Source*: Tay-Koay Seiw Luan, 1997.)

A variation on this theme came from a school in the Socrates Project 'Evaluating Quality in School Education' (MacBeath *et al.*, 1999). Students armed with tape recorders dropped into classes at random and picked a student to question about her learning at that moment. At that school it also became apparent that many students lacked the conceptual language to describe their learning or thinking. The awareness of this is a valuable starting-point for growth.

Shadowing

Shadowing is a simple, economic, but potentially rich technique for getting an insight into a slice of school or classroom life. In a secondary school, for example, an individual student may be followed over the course of a day, as she moves from class to class, through breaks, lunch hour, games or library times. The intention is to 'see' the school through the eyes of the student. Shadowing can be done by a teacher, headteacher, parent, member of the governing body, a teacher in training, or a school student. There are three key considerations to bear in mind:

1. The presence of the shadower will affect how typical the school day is. The status of the shadower will have the deepest impact. A headteacher is unlikely to see a representative example of a lesson or school day. A school student is likely to create less 'disturbance' to routine events.
2. Seeing the familiar as unfamiliar may be more difficult for a school student immersed day to day in the environment of the school.

3 A clear task focus and preparation are critical. Unfocused observation is likely to bring minimal returns. Things to look for and questions to ask are crucial. A set of questions can be provided for the shadower to debrief the student at regular intervals.

Shadowing may be of a student, a teacher, a headteacher, a member of office or technical staff, or a member of the governing body.

The purpose and audience for the results needs to be clear beforehand. The audience may, for example, be the senior management team, the whole staff, parents or a joint parent–teacher meeting.

Interviews

Interviewing is one of the most common ways of gathering data. It is potentially the richest source but also the most time-consuming and complex. For school self-evaluation, consideration has to be given to the following:

- What is the purpose?
- Who will be involved?
- How can representativeness be assured?
- What is the best – individual or group interview?
- How long will each interview last?
- Who will conduct the interviews?
- How will confidentiality or anonymity be ensured?
- Where will interviews be held?
- How will they be recorded (tape or notes?)
- Will they be structured, semi-structured or open-ended?
- Who will analyse the data?
- What will the costs be?
- Will the return repay the investment of time, energy and resources?
- Are there other more economical alternatives?

Many of these seem obvious and even trivial questions, yet simple things like time and place are extremely important. The setting may be comfortable, relaxing, or intimidating to the interviewee. The headteacher's study, for example, may inhibit any frank discussion. Time, too, has to be allowed for people to establish trust and gradually express their real feelings. In the right setting and with the right climate the success of the interview also then relies on the skills of the interviewer in allowing time for reflection, prompting and probing sensitively, reading and responding to the feelings of the interviewee.

With children, especially younger ones, it is often preferable to have a group interview with three or more present. This helps to ease the tension for children who find the interview situation unfamiliar and threatening. They'll feel more free to speak if there are others of their age present. As with all of these techniques, piloting beforehand is important in testing and refining the interview protocol.

Focus groups

Focus groups are a more economical way of getting a great deal of information quickly. The focus group may, theoretically, be any size. If it is a face-to-face group it will probably be around ten or twelve people, chosen to represent different viewpoints, age or status. In a school it might consist of students of different ages and both sexes. Or it might be a mixture of students and teachers. Its function is to provide information in as open and honest way as possible, allowing the group to debate and distil the issues, arriving at consensus where there is genuine agreement and identifying differences where those differences are significant.

A school focus group might be asked to take a broad view of the organisation as a whole or to provide feedback on specific aspects such as homework, discipline, learning and teaching, parent meetings or professional development, for example. Running the group, keeping it on task, creating the right kind of climate and encouraging participation require expert skills, and it may be best for a school to secure the services of an outside person for this purpose unless it has an inside person with that role and relevant expertise.

Profiling

Focus groups may provide the forum for the use of profiling techniques. These can take many forms and be used in many different ways and for different purposes. The profile consists of a set of criteria (perhaps ten or a dozen) which people use to evaluate the school as a whole or specific aspects of it. A good example of the profile comes from the Socrates Project 'Evaluating Quality in School Education'. In this project the 101 participating schools all used the same profile of twelve characteristics as reproduced in Figure 8.18. Four groups of stakeholders (students, parents, teachers and governing bodies) were involved in assessing their school on each of the twelve categories using a four-point scale plus a judgement on improvement, decline or

	++	+	–	––	↗	↔	↘
Outcomes							
Academic achievement							
Personal and social development							
Student destinations							
Process at classroom level							
Time for learning							
Quality of learning and teaching							
Support for learning difficulties							
Process at school level							
School as a learning place							
School as a social place							
School as a professional place							
Environment							
School and home							
School and community							
School and work							

Figure 8.18: The school self-evaluation profile

stability. Each of the four groups then sent two of their members to a school evaluation group whose task it was to reach consensus on the twelve criteria. This proved in most cases to be difficult but, in the process of discussion and negotiation, brought to the surface clear differences of opinion. It required people to listen more carefully to perspectives and experiences quite different from their own.

Following the evaluation by the group, a number of key areas for further evaluation or action were agreed on. The profiling instrument (Figure 8.18) provides a target over the course of the next year for the school to work towards.

Critical incident analysis

The critical incident analysis focuses on a micro-event in the life of a school. It might be a confrontation between a teacher and student, a complaint from a parent, or a communication difficulty in a senior management meeting. The purpose of the analysis is to unpack the incident in as much detail and depth as possible to throw light on school procedures, attitudes or capacity to handle conflict. The ultimate purpose is to identify what could be done to avoid a similar happening in the future or, more positively, to develop more effective communication, a more resilient culture or more widely agreed norms. Figure 8.19 gives an example from an analysis by a group of fifteen-year-old students of a disciplinary incident in one classroom.

The value of the analysis is not only in reaching a deeper level of shared insight, but in examining points at which action could have been taken to avert the escalation of trouble. The student group were able to identify a number of

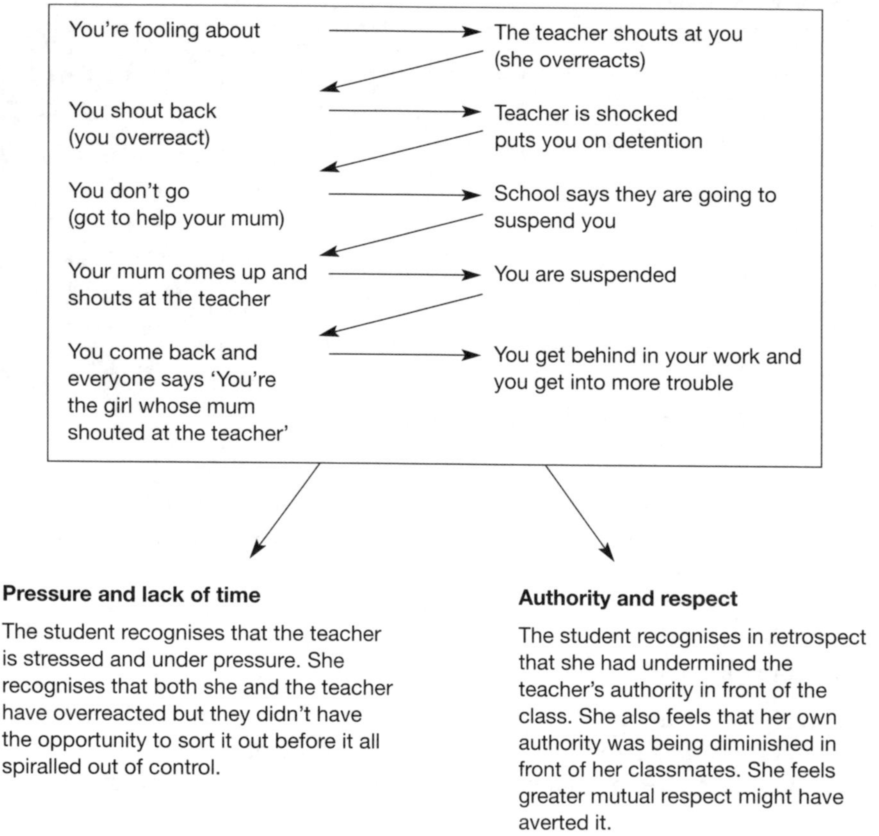
You're fooling about
The teacher shouts at you (she overreacts)
You shout back (you overreact)
Teacher is shocked puts you on detention
You don't go (got to help your mum)
School says they are going to suspend you
Your mum comes up and shouts at the teacher
You are suspended
You come back and everyone says 'You're the girl whose mum shouted at the teacher'
You get behind in your work and you get into more trouble
Pressure and lack of time
The student recognises that the teacher is stressed and under pressure. She recognises that both she and the teacher have overreacted but they didn't have the opportunity to sort it out before it all spiralled out of control.
Authority and respect
The student recognises in retrospect that she had undermined the teacher's authority in front of the class. She also feels that her own authority was being diminished in front of her classmates. She feels greater mutual respect might have averted it.

Figure 8.19: A spiral of trouble

things that could have been done by the student herself, by other students or by the teacher. The critical incident analysis is also useful to the teacher who is better equipped to deal with the situation next time and has a common reference point with the class.

In conclusion

The quality of leadership in a school is tested most stringently by the nature and experience of a school's day-to-day life. Schools have at their disposal a large array of tools and strategies for self-evaluation which, when used systematically and with thought as to purpose and audience, can go beyond awareness-raising to a wider sharing of leadership.

Before embarking on pupil shadowing

- is it appropriate to stay with the pupil (teacher/head) during break and lunchtime?
- should the teacher/pupil match be the same sex and ethnicity?
- how do you communicate to all staff concerned that the purpose of the exercise is not to check on them?
- what do you report back to staff and pupils on your experience?
- how do you ensure that the exercise is used to improve school practice?

While pupil tracking

- what sort of range of teaching styles does your pupil encounter during her day, e.g. whole class/group work?
- does the content of the curriculum in any way reflect her experiences or heritage?
- is she encouraged to be an independent and responsible learner?
- does she have an opportunity to participate in oral work in the classroom? If so, does she do so?
- how many interactions does she have with teachers during the day? are they generally positive? is she called by name in the classroom or corridors?
- how does the pupil relate to her peer group?

After pupil tracking

- if relevant, what was the extent and effectiveness of learning support?
- were there connections between subject areas? were they made apparent to the pupil?
- did the day appear to have coherence?
- did the pupil receive mixed messages from the different adults she encountered?
- how did she spend her day out of classroom time? was there somewhere appropriate for her to go? were the corridors safe?
- what did she think of her schooling in general and the day you have observed in particular?

Guidelines for shadowing or 'tracking'

Divide participants into small groups (5 – 6 per group). Assign them the perspective of students, tutors, parents. Ask them to agree on five key indicators of a good school (or classroom, or learning). (10 minutes)

Create three new mixed groups of three (one from each) or group of six (two from each).

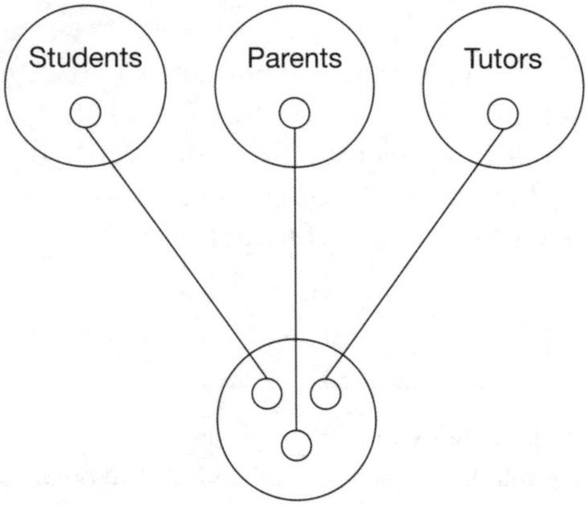

Task

Agree on seven key indicators. Discuss how evidence might be gathered as to the achievement of these. Discuss some kinds of instruments which might be used. (20 minutes)

Plenary

Facilitator brings ideas together. Compiles common list of indicators. Probes, challenges on precision, focus, measurability. Discusses notions of qualitative and quantitative approaches. Clears up common confusion over the two (see suggested reading).

School speaking for themselves – the process

Consider the main purpose, or purposes, of different kinds of evaluation, what form they take and the audience for whom they are intended.

Purpose	*Form*	*Audience*
political		
accountability		
diagnostic		
formative or developmental		
marketing or public relations		
other		

Evaluation – a question of purpose

References

■ ■ ■

Acker, S. (ed.) (1989) *Teachers, Gender and Careers*, London: Falmer.

Adler, S., Laney, J. and Packer, M. (1993) *Managing Women*, Buckingham: Open University Press.

Arygris, C. and Schön, D. (1978) *Organisational Learning: A theory of action perspective*, Reading, MA: Addison Wesley.

Barber, M. and Brighouse, T. (1992) *Partners in Change: Enhancing the teaching profession*, London: IPPR.

Bennett, A.E., Bryk, A.S., Easton, J.Q., Kerbow, D., Luppescu, S. and Sebring, P. (1992) *Charting Reform: The principal's perspective*, Chicago: Consortium on Chicago School Research.

Bennis, W. (1997) *Organizing Genius: The secrets of creative collaboration*, London: Nicholas Brealey.

Bennis, W. and Nanus, B. (1985) *Leaders: the strategies for taking charge*, New York: Harper & Row.

Bernstein, B. (1970) 'Education cannot compensate for society', *New Society*, 387, 344–47.

Binney, G. and Williams, W. (1997) *Leaning into the Future: Changing the way people change organisations*, London: Nicholas Brealey.

Black, J. (1994) *Mindsfore*, London: Thorsons.

Bohm, D. (1983) *Wholeness and the Implicate Order*, New York: Ark Paperbacks.

Bolman, L.G. and Deal, T.E. (1991) *Reframing Organisations: Artistry, choice and leadership*, San Francisco, CA: Jossey-Bass.

Boothroyd, C., Fitz-Gibbon, C., McNicholas, J., Thompson, M., Stern, E. and Wragg, T. (1997) *A Better System of Inspection?* Northumberland: OFSTIN.

Boylett, I. and Finlay, D. (1996) 'Corporate governance and the school headteacher', *Public Money and Management*, April–June, pp. 31–38.

Brighouse, T. and Woods, D. (1999) *How to Improve Your School*, London: Routledge.

Cave, E. and Wilkinson, C. (1997) in Kydd, L., Crawford, M. and Riches, C. (eds.) *Professional Development for Educational Management*, Buckingham: Open Unversity Press.

Coleman, P. (1998) *Parent, Student and Teacher Collaboration: The power of three*, London: Paul Chapman.

Cooperrider and Srivasta (1999) quoted in Brighouse, T. and Woods, D. (1999) *How to Improve your School*, London: Routledge.

Cornog, G. (1970) 'To care and not to care', in Ryan, K. *Don't Smile Until Christmas*, Chicago: University of Chicago Press, pp. 1–24.

Covey, S. (1995) *Principle-centred Leadership*, New York: Houghton Mifflin.

Covey, S. (1989) *The Seven Habits of Highly Effective People*, New York: Simon and Schuster.

Covey, S. and Merrill, R.A. (1994) *First Things First*, New York: Simon & Schuster.

Csikszentmihalyi, M. (1990) *Flow: the psychology of optimal experience*, New York: Harper Perennial.

De Lyon, H. and Widdowson Migniuolo, F. (eds.) (1989) '"Miss is a Lesbian": The Experience of a White Lesbian Teacher in a Boys School' in *Women Teachers. Issues and Experiences*, Buckingham: Open University Press.

Dempster, N. and Logan, L. (1998) in MacBeath, J. (ed.) *Effective School Leadership: Responding to change*, London, Paul Chapman.
Dempster, N. and Mahony, P. (1998) in MacBeath, J. (ed.) *Effective School Leadership: Responding to change*, London, Paul Chapman.
Dimock, C. (1996) 'Dilemmas for school leaders and administrators in restructuring,' in Leithwood, K., Chapman, J., Coson, D., Hallinger, P. and Hart, A. (eds.) *International Handbook of School Leadership and Administration*, Vol. 1, Dordrecht: Kluwer.
Earley, P. (ed.) (1998) *School Improvement after Inspection? School and LEA Responses*, London: Paul Chapman.
Epstein, D. (ed.) (1994) *Challenging Lesbian and Gay Inequalities in Education*, Buckingham: Open University Press.
Epstein, D. and Johnson, R. (1998) *Schooling Sexualities*, Buckingham: Open University Press.
Evetts, J. (1994) *Becoming a Secondary Headteacher*, London: Cassell.
Feuerstein, R., Rand, Y., Hoffman, M.A. and Miller, R. (1980) *Instrumental Enrichment: An intervention programme for cognitive modifiability*, Baltimore, MD, University Park Press.
Fielding, M. (1998) 'Making a difference', paper presented at International Congress on School Effectiveness and School Improvement, Manchester, January.
Franks, S. (1999) *Having None of It. Women, Men and the Future of Work*, London: Grant.
Fullan, M. (1997a) *What's Worth Fighting for in the Principalship?*, Mississauga: Ontario Teachers' Federation.
Fullan, M. (1997b) 'Emotion and hope: constructive concepts for complex times', in Hargreaves, A. (ed.) *Positive Change for School Success*, Alexandria, VA: ASCD 1997 Yearbook.
Galton, M., Hargreaves, L. and Pell, A. (1997) *Class Size, Teaching and Pupil Achievement*, London: National Union of Teachers.
Gardner, H. (1997) *Leading Minds: An anatomy of leadership*, London: HarperCollins.
Gilligan, C. (1982) *In a Different Voice*, Cambridge, MA: Harvard University Press.
Goleman, D. (1996) *Emotional Intelligence*, London: Bloomsbury.
Grace, G. (1995) *School Leadership, Beyond Education Management*, London: Falmer.
Gray, J. and Wilcox, B. (eds.) (1995) *Good School, Bad School: Evaluating performance and encouraging improvement*. Buckingham: Open University Press.
HM Inspectors of Schools, Audit Unit (1999) *Quality and Standards in Scottish Schools*, Scottish Office Education and Industry Department, Edinburgh, HMSO.
HM Inspectors of Schools, Audit Unit (1997) *How Good is Our School?*, Scottish Office Education and Industry Department, Edinburgh, HMSO.
Hackman, J.R. and Oldham, G. (1976) 'Motivation through the design of work: A test of theory', *Organisational Behaviour and Human Performance*, 16 (2), 250–79.
Hall, G. and Hord, S. (1987) *Change in Schools: Facilitating the process*, Albany, New York: State University of New York Press.
Hall, V. (1996) *Dancing on the Ceiling. A study of women managers in education*, London: Paul Chapman.
Hampden-Turner, C. and Trompenaars, L. (1993) *The Seven Cultures of Capitalism*, New York: Doubleday.
Hannon, P. (1993) 'Conditions of learning at home and in school', in *Ruling the Margins*, London: Institute of Education, University of North London.
Hargreaves, A. (1995) *Changing Teachers, Changing Times*, London: Cassell.

Hargreaves, D. (1999) Creative Professionalism: The role of teachers in the knowledge society, London: *DEMOS*, pp. 29–32.

Hargreaves, D. (1997) 'Equipped for Life', ESRC paper, Cambridge: School of Education, University of Cambridge.

Hargreaves, D.H. (1998) 'The knowledge creating school', Paper delivered at the *British Educational Research Association*, Queen's University, Belfast: August.

Heifetz, R.A. (1994) *Leadership Without Easy Answers*, Cambridge, MA: Harvard University Press.

Herbert, C. (1992) *Sexual Harassment in Schools. A guide for teachers*, London: David Fulton.

Herndon, J. (1968) *The Way it Spozed to Be*, New York, Wiley.

Hertzler, J.O. (1940) 'Crises and Dictatorships', *American Sociological Review*, 4, 157–69.

Hill, N. (1928) *Secrets of Success*, New York: Schuster.

House, E. (1973) *School Evaluation: The politics and process*, San Francisco: McCutchan Publishing.

Illich, I. (1971) *Deschooling Society*, New York: Harper and Row.

Jarvis, P. (1997) 'Learning practical knowledge', in Kydd, L., Crawford, M. and Riches, C. (eds.) (1997) *Professional Development for Educational Management*, Buckingham: Open University Press, pp. 26–36.

Kotter, J.P. (1996) *Leading Change*, Boston, MA: Harvard Business School Press.

Kotulak, R. (1996) *Inside the Brain: Revolutionary discoveries of how the mind works*, Kansas City: Andrews McMeel.

Kydd, L., Crawford, M. and Riches, C. (1997) *Professional Development for Educational Management*, Buckingham: Open University Press.

Leithwood, K. (1999) *Educational Accountability: The state of the art*, Gütersloh: Bertlesmann Foundation.

MacBeath, J. (1999) *Schools Must Speak for Themselves*, London: Routledge.

MacBeath, J. (1998) (ed.) *Effective School Leadership: Responding to change*, London: Paul Chapman.

MacBeath, J., Boyd, B., Rand, J. and Bell, S. (1996) *Schools Speak for Themselves*, London: National Union of Teachers.

MacBeath, J., Kruchov, C. and Riley, K. (1994) *Images of Leadership*, Glasgow: University of Strathclyde.

MacBeath, J., Mearns, D. and Smith, M. (1986) *Home from School*, Scottish Education Department, Glasgow: Jordanhill College.

MacBeath, J., Meuret, D., Schratz, M. and Jakobsen, L. (1999) *Evaluating Quality in School Education*, Brussels. European Commission.

MacBeath, J. and Mortimer, P. (1994) 'Improving School Effectiveness: A Scottish Approach', paper presented to the British Educational Research Association annual conference, Oxford University, September.

Macdonald, A. (1998) 'Postscript', in MacBeath, J. (ed.) *Effective School Leadership: Responding to change*, London: Paul Chapman.

Macdonald, J. (1989) 'When outsiders try to change schools from the inside', *Phi Delta Kappan*, 71 (3), 208.

MacGilchrist, B., Mortimore, P., Savage, J. and Beresford, C. (1995) *Planning Matters*, London: Paul Chapman.

Marshall, J. (1984) *Women Managers. Travellers in a Male World*, Chichester: Wiley.

Martin, P. (1997) *The Sickening Mind*, London: Flamingo.

Mead, M. (1949 rpt 1981) *Male and Female: A study of the sexes in a changing world*, Harmondsworth: Penguin.

Mintzberg, H. (1994) *The Rise and Fall of Strategic Planning*, New York: Prentice Hall.
Mortimore, J. and Mortimore, P. (1991) *The Secondary Head: Roles, Responsibilities and Reflections*, London: Paul Chapman.
Mortimore, P. and Whitty, G. (1999) 'Can school improvement overcome the effects of disadvantage', in Cox, T. *Combatting Educational Disadvantage*, London: Falmer.
Myers, K. (1995–1998) 'Talking Heads', series of articles in the *Times Educational Supplement*, London.
Nias, J., Southworth, G. and Yeomans, R. (1989) *Staff Relationships in a Primary School: A study of organisational cultures*, London: Cassell.
Office of Standards in Education (1995) *New Framework for School Inspections*, London: Department for Education and Employment.
Ouston, J., Fidler, B. and Earley, P. (1998) 'The educational accountability of schools in England and Wales', *Educational Policy*, 12 (1), 111–23.
Ozga, J. and Walker, L. (1999) 'In the company of men', in Whitehead, S. and Moodey, R. (eds.) *Transforming Managers: Engendering Change in the Public Sector*, London: Taylor and Francis.
Paul, R. (1996) Dialogical thinking: Critical thought essential to the acquisition of ritual knowledge and passions, unpublished seminar paper, University of Glasgow.
Pinker, S. (1998) *How the Mind Works*, London: Penguin Books.
Rafferty, F. (1995) 'Football governors attacked by the head', *Times Educational Supplement*, 2 June.
Rallis, S.F. (1988) *Dynamic Teachers: Leaders of change*, Thousand Oaks, California: Corwin Press.
Reay, D. (1993) 'He doesn't like you Miss: Working with boys in an infant classroom', in Claire, H., Maybin, J. and Swann, J. *Equality Matters: Case studies from the primary school*, Clevedon: Multilingual Matters.
Reeves, J. and Dempster, N. (1998) 'Developing Effective School Leaders', in MacBeath, J. (ed.) *Effective School Leadership: Responding to change*, London: Paul Chapman.
Reeves, J. and MacGilchrist, B. (1997) 'Gauging the impact of improvement strategies'. *Paper presented at the British Educational Research Association, University of York*, York: September.
Riehl, C. and Lee, V.E. (1995) 'Gender, Organisation and Leadership', in Leithwood, K. *et al.* (eds.) *International Handbook of Educational Leadership and Administration*, Dordrecht: Kluwer.
Rosenblum, S., Louis, K.S. and Rossmiller, R. (1994) 'School leadership and teacher quality of work life', in Murphy, J. and Louis, K.S. (eds.) *Reshaping the Principalship*, Newbury Park: Corwin Press.
Ross, S. (1995) 'Using ethos indicators in a primary school', *Managing Schools Today*, pp. 26–30.
Rutter, M., Maughan, B., Mortimore, P. and Ouston, J. (1979). *Fifteen Thousand Hours: Secondary schools and their effects on children*, Cambridge, MA: Harvard University Press.
Salomon, G. and Perkins, D. (1998) 'Individual and social aspects of learning', *Review of Research in Education*, 23.
Schratz, M. and Steiner-Löffler, U. (1998) *Die Lemende Schule*, Weinheim: Beltz Verlag.
Scottish Office Education and Industry Department (1998) *Standards and Quality 1995–1998*, A Report by HM Inspectors of Schools, The Audit Unit, Edinburgh: SOEID.

Senge, P. (1992) *The Fifth Discipline: The art and practice of the learning organisation*, Sydney: Random House.

Sergiovanni, T. (1998) 'Leadership as pedagogy, capital development and school effectiveness', *International Journal of Leadership in Education*, 1 (1), 37.

Sergiovanni, T.J. (1992) *Moral Leadership: Getting to the heart of school improvement*, San Francisco, LA: Jossey-Bass.

Shakeshaft, C. (1989) *Women in Education Administration*, New York: Sage.

Simkins, T., Ellison, L. and Garrett, V. (1992) 'Beyond market and managerialism? Education management in a new context', in Simkins, T. *et al. Implementing Educational Reform: The early lessons*, Harlow: Longman.

Sobel, D. (1997) *Longitude*, London: Fourth Estate.

Southworth, G. (1995) *Looking into Primary Headship: A research based interpretation*, London: Falmer.

Spencer, L. (1978) *Soft Skill Competencies*, New York: McBer.

Spencer, L.M. and Spencer, S.M. (1993) *Competence at Work: Models for superior performance*, New York: Wiley.

Steiner-Löffler, U. (1996) 'Pupils evaluate school culture: a photographic approach', Paper presented at the European Educational Research Association, Seville, September.

Tay-Koay Seiw Luan (1997) 'Students' reports of their cognitive processes and level of understanding during regular classroom instruction', in Tan, J., Gopi, S., Nathan and Kam, Ho Wah. *Education in Singapore*, Singapore: Prentice Hall, pp. 187–204.

Tiana, A., Scheerens, J., MacBeath, J., Thomas, S. and Smees, S. (1999) *Innovative Approaches to Evaluation*, Brussels: European Commission Report.

Trenchard, L. and Warren, H. (1984) *Something to Tell You*, London: Gay Teenagers' Group.

'V' (1996) *The Mafia Manager*, New York: St. Martin's Griffin.

Varlaam, A., Nuttall, D. and Walker, A. (1992) *What Makes Teachers Tick? A survey of teacher morale and motivation*, Clare Market Papers No. 4, Centre for Education Research, LSE.

Walkerdine, V. (1987) 'Sex, Power and Pedagogy', in Arnot, M., Weiner, M. and G. *Gender and the Politics of Schooling*, London: Hutchinson in association with the Open University.

Waller, W. (1932) *The Sociology of Teaching*, Wiley: London and New York.

Wheatley, M. (1994) *Leadership and the New Science*, New York: Berrett–Koehler.

Wilcox, B. and Gray, J. (1996) *Inspecting Schools*, Buckingham: Open University Press.

Wilhite, M. and Basnet, L. (1999) 'Teaching excellence', *POD Network Newsletter*, 10 (5).

Winkley, D. (1989) 'An analytical view of primary school leadership', *School Organisation*, 3 (1).

Wragg, T. (1998) 'What Do We Really Mean by Incompetent Teachers?', *Parliamentary Brief*, p. 52.

Index

■ ■ ■